P9-ELO-355

ONE MAN'S EXTRAORDINARY
STORY OF SURVIVAL

OF WILL

GREY*S*TONE BOOKS
Douglas & McIntyre Publishing Group
Vancouver / Toronto / Berkeley

Copyright © 2004 by Warren Macdonald

An earlier edition of this book was published in Australia and New Zealand
by Hardie Grant Books under the title *One Step Beyond.*

07 08 09 10   8 7 6 5

All rights reserved. No part of this book may be reproduced, stored in
a retrieval system or transmitted, in any form or by any means, without
the prior written consent of the publisher or a licence from The Canadian
Copyright Licensing Agency (Access Copyright). For a copyright licence, visit
www.accesscopyright.ca or call toll free to 1-800-893-5777.

Greystone Books
A division of Douglas & McIntyre Ltd.
2323 Quebec Street, Suite 201
Vancouver, British Columbia
Canada V5T 4S7
www.greystonebooks.com

National Library of Canada Cataloguing in Publication Data
Macdonald, Warren, 1965–

A test of will : one man's extraordinary story of survival / Warren Macdonald.

ISBN-13: 978-1-55365-064-5 · ISBN-10: 1-55365-064-6

1. Macdonald, Warren, 1965– 2. Mountaineering accidents—
Queensland—Bowen, Mount. 3. Mountaineers—Australia—Biography.
4. Amputees—Biography. I. Title.
GV199.92.M32A3 2004   796.5'22'092   C2004-902690-9

Library of Congress information is available upon request

Editing by Anne Rose
Cover and interior design by Jessica Sullivan
Cover photograph by Brad Wrobleski
Map by Stuart Daniel/Starshell Maps
Printed and bound in Canada by Friesens
Printed on acid-free paper that is forest-friendly (100% post-consumer
recycled paper) and has been processed chlorine free
Distributed in the U.S. by Publishers Group West

For Matthew, Jordan, Samantha, Riley, Rebecca and Tara;
when they are old enough to understand.

CONTENTS

part I THE ROAD LESS TRAVELED   1

part II THE WILL TO LIVE   111

part III THE RECLAMATION   145

EPILOGUE   193

ACKNOWLEDGMENTS   197

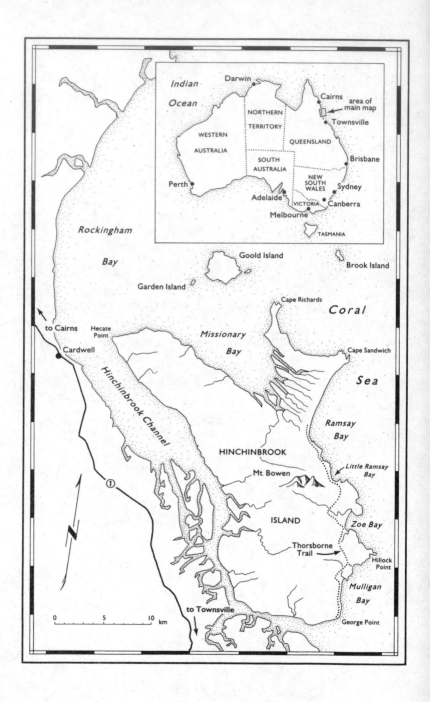

Indian
Ocean

Darwin

Cairns
area of
main map

Townsville

NORTHERN
TERRITORY

WESTERN

AUSTRALIA

QUEENSLAND

Brisbane

SOUTH
AUSTRALIA

NEW
SOUTH
WALES

Sydney

Perth

Adelaide

VICTORIA Canberra

Melbourne

TASMANIA

Rockingham

Bay

Goold Island

Brook Island

Garden Island

Cape Richards

Coral

to Cairns

Hecate
Point

Missionary

Bay

Cape Sandwich

Cardwell

Sea

Hinchinbrook Channel

Ramsay
Bay

HINCHINBROOK

Little Ramsay
Bay

Mt Bowen

①

ISLAND

Zoe Bay

Thorsborne
Trail

Hillock
Point

Mulligan
Bay

0   5   10 km

to Townsville

George Point

PART I

THE ROAD
LESS TRAVELED

God be with those who explore in the cause of understanding; whose search takes them far from what is familiar and comfortable and leads them into danger or terrifying loneliness. Let us try to understand their sometimes strange or difficult ways; their confronting or unusual language; the uncommon life of their emotions, for they have been affected and shaped and changed by their struggle at the frontiers of a wild darkness, just as we may be affected, shaped and changed by the insights they bring back to us. Bless them with strength and peace. Amen.

MICHAEL LEUNIG

The Final Step

Stepping ever so carefully, edging forward in the dark, I make my way across the narrow creek bed. With no recent rain, it's almost dry, apart from a thin trickle down the center, the sound of which is all that's to be heard—that, and the rustling of Geert settling into his sleeping bag behind me.

My bare feet probing forward, I pull back from contact with the cool moss tempting me to slide across its surface, and search instead for dry rock before shifting my weight forward. A few more steps and I'm across, reaching out in the dark for the granite bank I need to climb if I'm going to get any distance from this creek. This is turning into a bit of a mission just to go for a leak, but having had more than one dose of giardia, I'm not about to break the golden rule and urinate anywhere near the water. (So many seemingly pristine watercourses are now infected with this intestinal bug, which is transmitted through human waste and usually only clears up with a course of antibiotics.) Hikers should always go at least 50 meters (164 feet) from any creek or stream, double that if they've got other intentions. But once over this embankment, I should be far enough away. My groping fingers, feeling their way across the rock's surface, discover a crack, easily deep enough for me to get a good hold. I follow it upward to a comfortable height and begin searching with my right hand for a second hold. OK. *So far, so good.*

Raising my left leg, I place the foot in several positions, rocking forward slightly, searching for the right balance between hands and feet. Geert is silent now, settled into his bag under the cover of my thin nylon tarp. The soft murmur of mountain juices bubbling, descending toward the sea, their journey just begun, is now the only sound in the still of night. Confident of my hold, I rock forward on my left leg, simultaneously pulling up with my left hand. Suddenly, there's a loud crack, and in that split second, the world beneath me gives way.

ANOTHER CRACK (my pelvis fracturing, I learn later), then a crying out—no words, just a groan, forced out as I tense on impact, my diaphragm pushed upward, hard. Pain comes instantly, a sharp burning pain, shooting up from my lower body. I've got no idea what's happened at first—the actual fall, even now, gone from my memory, removed perhaps to protect me. I can't move! Something's on top of me!—crushing me against the creek bed below. *What's happening! What the fuck's going on!?* I reach down frantically and feel cold, rough stone. Then, comprehension as to what's happened hits me like a steam train and I push desperately with all my might. Nothing moves—the pain unbearable in my legs and pelvis, searing and grinding, like nothing I have felt before—as I struggle violently from side to side, trying to wriggle free.

"Fuck!" I cry out in agony. "Grab the flashlight!"

Geert is quickly unzipping his sleeping bag. "What? What's happened? Warren, are you all right?"

"Mate, quick, bring the flashlight!" I breathe out heavily as I struggle to push myself free.

Scrambling quickly across the slimy rocks, flashlight beam darting wildly, Geert is trying to make sense of the scene sporadically lit before him as he hurries closer.

"What's happened?" he shouts nervously, moving faster now. From the pain and urgency in my voice, and the sight unfolding in front of him as he reaches my side, it's clear to him that I'm in serious trouble.

"Aaagh, mate, here!" I plead. "Help me, push here!" He crouches quickly beside me, trying to gain footing on the slippery rock, feet splashing in the shallow water.

"All right, here?"

"Uuugh!" I groan, chest heaving with my fast, deep breathing. "Y-yeah, here, quick!"

"ok, push!" We both strain with all our combined strength, the kind of strength that comes from within, tapped from some primitive source deep in the mind that overrides all the warning signals, lets you force your body beyond its own pain barrier. I'm pushing so hard, I feel as if I'm almost pulling myself apart, trying to leave my trapped half behind, searing pain flaring in my upper thighs. Nothing moves and I cry out in despair, "Noooooooo!" My head and shoulders are thrown back in agony, the weight grinding down into my lap.

"Oh, faaark," I howl. "Go, again!"—my heaving voice full of urgency and desperation.

"OK, hang on, mate!" Once more, Geert frantically tries to get secure footing on the slimy rock before bracing himself to go again. "All right, go!"

We push again with all our might, faces grimacing in pain, muscles ready to explode. Pushing. Pushing. Pushing urgently. "C'monnnn!" I cry out.

It doesn't move. Not an inch. Not even a millimeter.

"Aaaaaaaagh! C'monnnnn!"

We're both still pushing, with whatever's left, pushing until there is nothing. I collapse backward, exhausted. Geert leans forward, head down, breathing hard.

OK. Calm, calm. Got to stay calm, I keep telling myself, over and over. Leaning forward, then back, trying to reduce the pain, get some kind of release from it. None comes. I sit there, face screwed up in agony, trying to come to grips with what's happened.

"Are you OK, mate?"

"Yep. Yeah, I think I'm OK." I take a deep breath. Somehow, very calmly, I set about giving Geert instructions as if I'm the foreman in charge of a building project.

"Mate, what we've got to do is"—another deep breath, grimacing in pain—"we need to get a branch, or a small tree." Another pause. "Something strong, for a lever."

"OK," says Geert, shining the flashlight along the bank quickly, forward and back, left and right.

"Over there, try over there," I say, as the beam lights up a stand of saplings, smooth-barked water gums rising above the sedge grass and stunted banksias lining the bank.

Eyes closed now, breathing deeply, trying to slow it down, trying to slow my heart, which feels like it's trying to burst out of my chest. C'mon, calm, calm. I keep telling myself, over and over, You've got to stay calm. All right!

Geert puts a hand on my shoulder reassuringly. "OK, mate, you're gonna be OK. I'll be as quick as I can, just hang in there, we'll get you out of here." As he heads toward the gums, I feel the first spots of rain. I look up into a black sky, the pitter-patter of raindrops increasing steadily. *No, not now. Please, not now!*

Time passes in slow motion as I lie slumped over the slab, waiting. I can hear Geert in the trees: wrenching and pulling, the swoosh-swoosh of leaves against each other as he whips a branch back and forth violently. I listen intently when he stops, picture him moving on to another, something he has more chance of breaking—willing him on in my mind, fighting the pain rising inside me, the fear. More swooshing, then *crack!* I pray he'll be quick. I can see the saber of light moving wildly up on the bank, throwing thousands of shadows all around the narrow gorge. Then he's heading back, a branch slung over one shoulder, the flashlight in the other hand throwing light across a now dangerously slick bed of stone. He slips, recovering well before continuing toward me.

Suddenly realizing my total vulnerability, my absolute reliance on another human being, sends more than a cold shiver down my spine. The thought hits me like an electric shock, my mind spinning so fast I can almost hear the whirr.

"Bloody hell, mate. Be careful. Just take your time." I start to shake.

"OK, where do you want it?"

"Under here. See where my leg is?" My left leg lies twisted under the granite slab, out of sight, but the right has only just been caught, one edge of the stone hanging over it by just 10 or 15 centimeters (4 or 6 inches). This makes the leg visible from the knee down, with a space beside it to introduce a lever. Geert slides the limb under the overhang, lifting until he finds the ceiling, his end now just under shoulder height.

"OK, are you ready?"

I've got both hands on the rock, ready to push. "Yeah, go for it!"

Bending his knees, Geert pushes up hard, grunting with effort, his whole body straining. I also push as hard as I can, trying to lift and slide myself out at once. The rock seems to shift momentarily, and I push with all my might.

"Faaaaaaaark!" I cry out as my bare skin shears under the rough stone, scraping horribly as I drag myself back a few centimeters. I double over in agony at the shift in weight from my pelvis to my upper thighs as

Geert, unable to hold the rock up any longer, lowers his end. It feels as if it's just fallen on me all over again.

I cry out "Again, quick!"—reeling from the pain. Responding instantly, Geert lifts again, grunting loudly, straining with the effort. I'm pushing with everything I've got, and more, but I still can't move. "Lift! Higher! Higher!" I'm wriggling frantically to break free, even more determined after my taste of success.

A *crack!* signals the end of our crowbar, but both of us are still pushing, unwilling to accept our failure. Geert keeps lifting until the branch is splintered like a punk rocker's mohawk.

"Faaaaaaaarkin' helllllll! Nooooooo!"

I start to feel really scared; it's raining hard now. For the first time, I think I might not be coming out of this. *No way! Don't even think about it!* But it's no good. I am still scared.

"We need another one."

Deep breath.

"Something stronger, maybe a small tree."

Another.

"You'll have to get it out of the ground somehow, mate."

Geert's nodding, kneeling beside me, "OK, hang in there, you're gonna be all right." With that, he's off, back downstream a little, then up the bank into the trees. I lie back, exhausted, shaking my head in pain and disbelief. It's raining harder now. I scan the sky for some sign of a clearing but there's nothing—just black. This can't be happening, it just cannot be happening. Time seems to be standing still, it feels like hours before he returns. It's probably more like 20 or 30 minutes.

Carrying a whole young tree stripped of leaves, carefully making his way across the bouldered creek bed, Geert looks exhausted. The butt of the sapling is split and splintered where he's had to wrestle it from its roots, using his Swiss Army knife to cut the tough, green fibers so unwilling to let go. Swiss Army knives were never designed to cut down trees. I can see now exactly which tool we need and, unfortunately, we don't have it.

Twelve months ago, while living in Tasmania, I completed a four-week introductory course in outdoor adventure tour guiding. One afternoon, our instructor, and since then a good friend of mine, Brian Hall, emptied the contents of his backpack onto the table. He then proceeded to describe the purpose and relevance of each item of equipment required for a typical overnight hike. Everything was pretty standard and familiar until he pulled out what looked like a very large pocketknife, except instead of a knife blade it had a 15- or 20-centimeter (6- or 8-inch) length of saw blade folded inside; the theory being that, in a situation where an injured party must be carried out, we would need to construct a stretcher. To do that requires a number of strong poles, and to get strong poles requires some type of cutting. (If you can break off the poles by hand, they're not going to be able to support somebody's weight safely for any length of time, especially if the rescue is over or through rough terrain.)

The fact that Geert has been able to break off these branches with his bare hands and a pocketknife means we don't have a hope in hell of lifting a rock—later estimated to weigh a ton—with one of them. It's not long before this one, too, gives way, slowly creaking before cracking and splintering under the pressure. *No-o-o-o! This can't be happening . . . it can't! I've got to get out!*

We both lie back, exhausted, a mixture of sweat and drizzling rain running down our faces. Leaning forward, I slump over the slab, like I'm sitting at a desk. In absolute despair, I feel like just giving up and sobbing into the stone. But something in me won't allow it. I snap back to reality, back into focus.

"There's got to be a better way. We've got to try something else. Let's just have a rest for a minute and think about this."

"Are you warm enough, Warren?" Geert asks, as he crosses the creek to the camp. Then, before I can answer, he adds, "Where's your sleeping bag?"

"Under the tarp, in the green stuff-sack," I reply. The mention of my sleeping bag reminds me that I should be in it now. Under the tarp. Fast asleep. Instead, I'm caught in a nightmare—a real one that I can't hope to just wake from and be OK. Watching Geert on the other side of the creek, under the tarp, I envy his freedom.

He returns with both our jackets and my sleeping bag, which he pulls from its cover. He helps me wrap it around my waist. The rain is getting heavier, and my woolen vest is now covered with droplets of water that soak in when I brush them. Putting the jacket on, I realize how cold I've become and appreciate the warmth it offers. And to think, I almost left it back with my car in Cardwell, somewhat suspicious of the merits of a waterproof, breathable material like Gore-Tex in the tropics. I decided at the last minute that it wouldn't take up much space, was relatively light, and, who knows, that it just might come in handy.

Geert puts on his own jacket, then sits down beside me and massages my shoulders to comfort me, making me feel so glad I'm not alone. Then, with cold, wet hands, he somehow rolls himself a smoke under the shelter of his jacket hood, anxious for the nicotine's calming effect. *Maybe he's one of those blokes who can roll a cigarette under water if he has to.*

I'm amazed at how clearly my mind is operating now, deliberate and calculating, recognizing the danger I'm in and the need for logical, positive action. *There must be a way!* I reason, and suddenly an idea springs forth.

"Rocks, we need some rocks, about this size [I shape a 25- to 30-centimeter (10- to 12-inch) square], down here, alongside my right leg."

While Geert gathers the stones, throwing them just to the side of me, I set them one on the other until I have a pillar reaching just below the ceiling of the mantle overhanging my right knee. Selecting a wedge-shaped stone and holding it in place with my left hand, I then belt it with another stone that I use as a hammer in my right. I get the wedge held in place, but can't hit it hard enough to accomplish anything more from my awkward position.

"Geert, give me a hand here. This might do it." I lean as far as I can to my left as he takes over the assault, driving the stone in as hard as possible.

"That's it. Keep going, mate. I like it. I like what I see here." The slab tilts slightly, easing the pressure on my right leg but transferring it instantly to my left. My whole body tenses with pain as my left leg is so badly crushed that it feels like it will split open.

"Mate! Stop!" I cry out, then fall back in agony. It seems like an eternity before I become accustomed to this latest version of pain—an incredible burning, as if the temperature has been turned up again. Fear descends like a dark cloud, the enormity of the situation now clear, my mind no longer refusing to accept the fact that I am trapped—trapped under a massive rock in the middle of a creek bed, in the pouring rain, eight hours' walk from the nearest trail, on a remote island. *This really can't be happening, can it?* Still struggling to accept my predicament, I notice something that makes me feel sick in the pit of my stomach, like I've just swallowed a large piece of ice. *The creek is rising.*

Whereas my ass was hardly touching the water in the beginning, I am now sitting in the middle of a rising creek with water swirling around me to mid-thigh. It has risen at least 7 to 10 centimeters (3 to 4 inches) since the rain began, and that was only a few hours ago. *No, it can't come up much further, can it? What am I going to do if it comes up higher?* I'm trying really hard to ignore that line of thought. *Mate, don't even think about it.*

"We need another branch, Geert. With you levering, and me using the rocks as a wedge, I reckon we can do it," I tell him hopefully. I don't dare mention the creek, but I'm sure he's aware of it. I don't want to accept it myself. As he walks away, I pull the sleeping bag in tighter around my waist. It's soaking wet now, sagging into my lap under the water. The rain has increased ten-fold, into a torrential downpour, and the sound of rushing water is getting louder by the minute as the level rises.

Geert seems to be gone forever, but when he returns it's with another young sapling that he has cracked by swinging from it and uprooting it. For another hour, we struggle in vain, Geert splashing around in the shin-deep water using the lever, while I fumble at piling the stones. They are under water now and my hands are freezing. I try to drive home a stone that is under the surface, but it's hopeless. We've both run out of energy, drained by our efforts, the rain destroying our spirits completely.

We can't move it; it's too heavy. The thought comes crashing down on my head like a ton of bricks. *I'm trapped.* Head down, eyes squeezed tightly shut, not wanting to hear myself say what must be said:

"You're gonna have to walk out, mate, as soon as it gets light."

The Decision

I feel so strange. Up until now I've been trying to convince myself that I'm not that badly hurt, that I am just trapped and I'll probably be fine as soon as I can get out of here: out from under the rock, out of the creek, and up onto the slab under the tarp where it is nice and dry. I can see it from where I'm pinned; it is only 3 meters (10 feet) away but it might as well be three hundred. I imagine dragging myself over to the tarp, trailing two broken legs behind me, and curling up in my sleeping bag to sleep; falling asleep and praying when I wake that it has all been just a bad dream.

I've always thought that, in a situation like this—an accident far from immediate medical help—I'd rather be the one that's injured than the guy left to carry out a rescue. I've never wanted to be the person pulling out all stops and taking responsibility for another person's well-being or, worse still, their very survival. Mainly because I know how much of a mission I would put myself on to get out in a hurry for help—to move as fast as I could while staying in control enough to not screw it up, to operate within my limits. *How wrong I've been! What a jerk!* I've never been badly injured before, not even at home, so how could I even have made that comparison?

Geert has one hell of a journey in front of him, and I know he is far from looking forward to it. He found it difficult on the way up, what with all the boulder hopping and bushwhacking; most of his life's hiking has been on well-marked trails. As well, the creek bed was dry on the way up; now, the entire boulder-strewn gully is slick with wet moss—each and every step will require absolute concentration. Conditions like this are so mentally exhausting, leaving you prone to mistakes, your heart skipping a beat every time you lose traction, unable to do anything but wait for the fall and hope it doesn't hurt too much. Something as easily acquired as a sprained ankle could now mean the difference between life and death. It dawns on me how much I'm relying on this guy I met only yesterday.

"Mate, you're going to have to be so careful. You have got to make it out, or I'm history."

Sitting down next to me now, his arm reassuringly around my shoulder as pelting rain pours down our faces and soaks us to the skin, Geert reminds me of the story he told earlier over our tortellini dinner. A story of how Peter, a friend he first met in Nepal, comforted him through a terrifying night in the Pyrenees Mountains. They had been caught in a storm high on the range bordering France and Spain. Somewhere along the way they'd lost the poles for the tent. Using their packs inside to create a space, then rocks around the outer edge to tension the nylon, they managed to protect themselves from what turned into a snowstorm. Water ran freely under the tent, and it wasn't long before they were both soaking wet. Geert, recovering from a recent injury, was unfit, the cold affecting him more than his companion. Peter worked all night to keep him warm, massaging him and feeding him hot soup, holding him close to retain body heat. Peter saved Geert's life that night, and it had obviously affected him deeply. His appreciation for Peter's actions shines through in his attention to me now, as he strokes my shoulders, reassuring me. I respond gratefully, feelings of awkwardness at his affection diminishing as quickly as they arise. I squeeze his hand in appreciation, the floodgates behind my eyes threatening to burst.

"You can do it, Warren. You're going to be OK. We can get you through this. People have survived far worse situations than this."

Have they? I don't know about that.

Although the rain has eased slightly, the level of water around my hips has not. "God, I'm getting cold."

"OK, mate, do you have some more clothes?" he asks, standing.

"In my pack, there's a bag with another shirt. And some socks," I reply. He returns with the bag, plus my Therm-a-rest (a thin, lightweight inflatable mattress). When I made up my bed earlier, I remember, I'd gotten some satisfaction out of preparing to sleep on a bed of stone—that I could add the experience to my collection of great Therm-a-rest campsite stories.

Still finding it difficult to accept my position, I watch as Geert crosses the creek to the tarp. Never has anything seemed so near and yet so far. He returns quickly with the Therm-a-rest, the only other shirt I have with me, and a pair of socks. I pull on the shirt over my woolen vest, then the Gore-Tex back over the top. Geert wraps the stuff-sack around my right foot, which is now under water. The socks I wear as gloves to try to keep my hands warm. They are already numb from the cold, even though I have kept rubbing them vigorously. Geert reorganizes my sleeping bag, wrapping it tightly around my waist as the current tries to drag it downstream. Luckily, it is an old bag, bought before manufacturers discovered Dry Loft (a Gore-Tex covering), so it is filled with Dacron. This synthetic material still manages to retain some warmth even when wet, whereas down bags become a soggy, cold lump.

All right, this is as good as it's going to get warmth wise. I am now wearing every item of clothing I have brought, and am constantly readjusting the waterlogged sleeping bag to keep the cold water from flowing between me and it.

Geert sets about collecting branches, some of which were tossed aside earlier after failing as levers. Setting them in place behind my back, he makes them into just the kind of support I need. This backrest allows me to sit, as opposed to either lying back, completely in the water, or folding forward over the slab. Once satisfied, Geert lays the Therma-rest across the support, increasing my comfort tremendously.

We begin to formulate a plan. Geert will leave at first light, not a minute before. Walking back down in the dark would be suicidal, and we both know that my life depends on his getting out. It is imperative that he descend with maximum care.

It will take at least eight hours for Geert to get back to the nearest campsite, at Little Ramsay Bay, where he will be greeted at the very least by a long drop toilet and a metal food locker, and at best by some fellow hikers. If he does run into other hikers, he will have to decide, depending on their number and experience, whether to send someone back up to me. Or he could send them on in his place to raise the alarm. The trip down will surely take its toll: it may be quicker to send someone fresher in his place. I pray silently that he is up to the challenges that lie ahead. I am filled with a sense of dread because, whatever happens, my situation is totally out of my control. But for now, Geert has to get some rest.

He'll need every ounce of energy he can muster tomorrow, and then some, when he'll face the most demanding and dangerous walk he's ever undertaken. Right now he is exhausted. I watch him crawl under the tarp into his warm, dry sleeping bag, sensing his feelings of guilt as he calls out to me across that small but immeasurable distance, "Are you all right, Warren?"

"Yeah, mate! I'm all right!" I reply, raising my voice to be heard above the drumming of rain that continues in earnest.

—— ESCAPE FROM PARADISE ——

As I threw my pack and boots into the car that April Sunday afternoon in 1997, three days before the accident, I felt more alive than I had in weeks. Living in Airlie Beach was difficult. Located halfway between Townsville and Cairns on the Queensland coast of northeastern Australia, Airlie acts as the gateway to the coast's Whitsunday Islands. Collectively, the Whitsundays encompass more than 70 tropical islands on the Great Barrier Reef, some inhabited, some not. (Of the developed islands, the most exclusive by far is Hayman.) But even life on a tropical island can be a challenge.

Working as a painter, I had just finished my second month-long contract on Hayman. Although all island contractors work hard, they party even harder, and I was leaving the island a physical wreck after riding the roller coaster that is life in the Whitsundays for seven months, with only periodic escapes into the nearby Conway National Park or to one of the less inhabited islands for a reality check. It was time to clear my head, get myself back down to earth after living life in top gear. I'd heard a fair bit about Hinchinbrook Island, located 450 kilometers (280 miles) north of Hayman, in particular the Thosbourne Trail that runs north to south the full length of the island's east coast. I figured three or four days would give me plenty of time to cover the 32-kilometer (20-mile) trail at a relaxed pace.

Having scribbled a quick note to my roommates, I couldn't get out the door fast enough. There's something about a road trip that I find really attractive—just getting up and going, with no fixed destination.

The romance of the road, they call it. The spirit of adventure. I've lived a fairly nomadic existence for such a long time that I become restless if life is too boring. And, for better or worse, I made the discovery many moons ago that it's usually only excuses we give ourselves that keep us from doing what we really want to do. I'd lost my fear of the unknown and had grown to enjoy the feeling of throwing my cards into the air to see what adventure they'd lead me to when they landed.

That Sunday, pulling out on to the highway just out of Proserpine, I felt ten feet tall—the stereo cranked up, endless sugar-cane fields blurring past the open windows on either side. The hot air lashed my face, keeping the sweat at bay. As the sun sank quickly into the horizon (as it does in North Queensland), the first stars began to speckle the sky. *Free again at last!* Hours passed as I chewed up kilometer after kilometer of highway, headlights blazing the trail ahead. It's a strange experience driving at night on an unfamiliar road—the countryside a mystery that won't be revealed till dawn.

Approaching Townsville, I was puzzled by the red lights high in the sky, forming a ring around the glowing town below. At first I thought they were aircraft. *Yeah, right!* Once I realized they were hilltop aircraft beacons, I pictured the landscape surrounding the town. I pulled off the road about an hour north of the city, happy with the distance I'd covered. After clearing a space in the back of the van, I rolled out my Therm-a-rest, then left it to self-inflate while I stepped out to take a leak. "Look at those stars!" I couldn't help remarking to myself. I climbed back into the van and fell asleep to the hum of highway traffic and the mosquitoes that had just found me.

Queensland is such a laid-back place to travel. Half an hour north of Ingham, just before Cardwell, I took a turnoff to Five Mile Creek. I'm not sure why; it just seemed like a good idea. Waiting for me at the end of a short gravel road was one of the best little swimming holes I've ever found so close to a highway; places like this are usually tucked away. With crystal clear water running over the smooth pebbled bottom, it was no more than 2 meters (6.5 feet) deep, but perfect for that wake-up swim in the morning. I left my clothes where they fell and dove off the bank, skin tingling in anticipation of the water's touch. I love the shudder that you get when you hit cold water; it courses through your body like a delicate electric shot, rejuvenating every cell. Swimming under the palms on the opposite bank, I smiled to myself, thinking, *It doesn't get much better than this.*

Arriving in Cardwell later that morning, I discovered that, yes, there would be a ferry leaving for Hinchinbrook Island—in about fifteen minutes. But the prospect of rushing into an organizational frenzy at such short notice didn't appeal to me. Instead, I decided to drive farther north for the day and explore the area around Mission Beach.

Back in Cardwell in time for breakfast the next morning, I hit the local supermarket for provisions to last me a week. Minutes after parking my car behind the ferry booking office, I was stepping on to the boat with a full pack and settling back in a seat, ready to enjoy the smooth ride across Missionary Bay to the island. I kept to myself the whole trip, soaking up the splendor of just being on the water, gazing in awe at the rugged peaks cutting into the horizon. No sooner had the boat moored than I shouldered my pack and left the other passengers swimming at the first beach we reached. The rest of the day I spent walking alone along the spectacular coast, the trail at times taking me inland, dropping into rain-forest-filled gullies before returning to a new bay each time.

Arriving at Little Ramsay Bay in the afternoon, I was greeted by the sight of a guy sitting on the sand, naked except for his headband, sketching the ocean scene before him. He looked completely relaxed and engrossed in his work, so I didn't greet him. Instead, I dropped my pack from my tired shoulders, stripped down, and waded into the cool water for my first swim of the day. Later, in the cool shade of the umbrella-like Calophyllum trees that dotted the dune, my neighbor introduced himself as Geert van Keulen, from Holland. He told me of his plan to climb to the summit of Mount Bowen, the island's highest peak, and had me interested immediately. I'd been admiring the rugged range forming the backbone of the island while swimming earlier, and I began calculating whether I could make the climb and still reach my scheduled ferry pickup at the island's southern end on the following Saturday.

"Give me ten minutes to think about it," I told him, but I had already made up my mind. The hike to the summit would be mostly bush-whacking, which appealed to my penchant for a challenge.

Waking on the beach before dawn, from the comfort of my sleeping bag I watched the sun rise. There's something almost magical about the sun traveling over the ocean, the way the first rays arc skyward from the horizon, while the glow of color spreads toward you across the water. I lay transfixed for a while, then wormed my way out of the bag. I stretched fully, right down to my toes, and allowed my whole body to soak up the golden rays till I could resist the urge no longer. Walking naked across the smooth, wet sand, my skin crawled with both anticipation and dread as the next wave rushed to greet me. Cool water flowed around my ankles. Stepping in further until the sea swelled around my thighs, I dove straight ahead into the next wave, staying under for a few seconds, savoring the exhilaration as my body kick-started into life. There's nothing better than waking up like that . . . well, almost nothing. When you've started the day with a dip in the ocean, you can do anything.

I swam for another ten minutes before leaving the water to stretch again back on the beach. The sunlight had hit the tops of the peaks now and was spreading slowly down their slopes. I couldn't get over how beautiful these mountains are: Mount Bowen, and "The Thumb" along-side, glowing gold. Geert was up now, so we had breakfast together before repacking our gear, both keen to get moving. OK, *let's get out there!*

Following the trail notes Geert had picked up in Townsville, we crossed the lagoon behind camp and made our way upstream until the water narrowed into a creek. We found it much easier going in the bush on the northern side at first. It had been cleared somewhat by a recent fire, so a lot of the tangly scrub was gone. But it didn't stay that way for long. Soon we were forced back into the creek bed, ducking under branches and jumping from rock to rock. Geert was finding it a lot tougher than I was. I found myself stopping and waiting a lot, trying not to get too far ahead. It's much harder walking at a slower pace than usual, and I found it difficult to stick with the "slowest sets the pace" rule. With that sort of walking I need to build up a momentum if I'm to travel quickly and efficiently. Moving slowly and stopping to balance after each move actually uses more energy. I tried to stay behind Geert as much as possible, letting him set the pace, but soon found myself back in front. After a couple of hours or so we stopped for a break, firing up the Trangia, our portable fuel stove, for a coffee.

"How are you traveling, mate?" I asked Geert.

"I'm finding it difficult to keep my balance. I've already fallen a couple of times."

"You'll be all right. Just take it easy. We're not in a big hurry. The notes say five hours but if it takes us a bit more, it won't matter."

I'd rarely felt more confident on my feet. I was bounding from rock to rock fearlessly, almost gracefully. It took me quite by surprise really. I hadn't carried a full pack any distance for at least eight or nine months and fully expected to take a couple of days to find my feet completely. And it's always hard to judge walking times as described in trail notes; everybody's got a different idea on what a steady pace is or how fast an experienced hiker covers different terrain. I knew we certainly weren't going to break any records but figured we must be about halfway to the campsite, which I presumed to be no more than a cleared space big enough to put up a tent. From there it should be an hour or so scrambling to the summit, leaving us with time to retrace our steps back to Little Ramsay Bay by late tomorrow afternoon.

We set off again, the sun high in the sky now, beating down on us through the canopy. In places water tumbled from one boulder to another. The further we went, the larger the boulders became, making for bigger and bigger pools. Unable to resist the temptation of another swim, I stripped down and eased into the cold mountain stream, taking a quick breath before plunging my head under. *Now this is what I call living!*

Geert arrived and sat on a rock beside the pool. I swam across to a small waterfall on the other side, pulling myself over slippery rocks while the force of the water tried to push me back. *No way*, I thought. *I'm going under there.* Behind the sheet of water was a space where the rock was undercut. I pushed myself through the screen, water pounding my neck and shoulders, and found I could breathe on the other side.

"Have a go, mate, it's excellent."

I had that exhilarating feeling of being in the wild, of being totally immersed in nature. This is what I'd come for—not so much to *see* the sights, but to *feel* them, to *be part of* them.

I slipped out of the water, treading carefully with my wet feet, then sat on a rock in the sun to dry off while Geert took my place. It was just what he needed: a bit of enjoyment, time out from our demanding hike to appreciate where we were and why we were here.

We continued for another hour before stopping for lunch.

"How much farther do you think it is, Warren?" Geert questioned.

"It's hard to say, but I don't think we could be more than an hour away now." It was about 1 PM, so we had been traveling for nearly five hours. "We must be pretty bloody close."

As we got higher, the creek narrowed, forcing us to crouch under the low branches reaching for their brothers on the other side to form a canopy. Several times we encountered a fork in the path where another stream joined ours. Some were just the rejoining point for our creek after a brief separation upstream. Others had begun separately, only now joining together for the journey to the sea. Most of these junctions had been clearly marked with rock cairns by walkers who'd passed before us—until I came to a junction with no guiding signs whatsoever. *We couldn't have passed the campsite, could we? Could I have just walked past it? And Geert also?*

The gully had filled with shadows as the sun dipped lower into the hills ahead of us. It was getting fairly late, and Geert was looking anxious, probably wondering what the hell he'd got himself into.

I was starting to feel anxious myself. We should have reached our destination. And if we were off track, we wouldn't have time to backtrack and find the right way. I had to be on the ferry at the south end of the island on Saturday, Geert on Sunday. Besides, I hadn't come across a spot big enough to put up a tent yet, given that the scrub was closed in tightly on both sides of the creek. I decided to climb out of the gully to get a better view, to see which would be the most likely direction to follow.

Struggling through waist-high shrubbery, treading on branches that kept my feet off the ground, I scrambled to the top of a rocky outcrop. Majestic peaks rose all around me, providing an amazing view. But even though I was standing on the top of the small rise I didn't have enough height to work out which course to follow. *Right or left?* Neither looked good, so I picked right. Leaving my pack with Geert, I then made my way up through what was now a very overgrown gully with a trickle of water running through it. I battled on for another few hundred meters (660 feet) with no sign of a cairn, before returning to Geert. *We couldn't be in the wrong gully, could we?*

"It must be up this way, mate." I motioned to the left as I joined Geert back at the fork. But I kept moving as he donned his pack to follow. I was desperate to find something now; I didn't want to let him down, to give him any doubt about my ability to deal with the situation. I wanted to forge ahead and return with the good news that all was well, the campsite was just upstream.

Jumping from rock to rock, I stopped often, scanning the scene for a cairn or some other sign. Half a kilometer upstream I came across a large, flat slab of rock, sloping into, and forming part of, the riverbed, which was dry at the moment but looked like it wouldn't stay that way if the water level rose. (Another golden rule, never camp in a riverbed.) It's far from ideal, I thought, but if worse comes to worst, it would have to do for an emergency campsite. If it did rain, and the river rose significantly, we'd just have to break camp and sit up in the bush for the night. We wouldn't get much sleep, but that wouldn't kill us.

Waiting for Geert to arrive, I became increasingly pissed off with myself. We definitely weren't where we were supposed to be. *Are you really enjoying this?* I asked myself. In a way, I was. Being caught out like we were reinforced my confidence as a hiker. It reminded me that, no matter what happened, I could survive. Take away another comfort—the campsite, in this case—and I'd still be OK. But we were running out of time.

"All right, mate, it's getting late. We're just going to have to make do with whatever space we can find to string up a tarp," I told Geert as he approached.

"This isn't the campsite?" he asked despairingly.

"No, it's not, mate. We should have come across it by now, though. I don't know what's happened. We must have taken a wrong fork somewhere. I can't see how, but I can't think of any other explanation," I said, almost apologetically. "If you wait here, I'm going to check a bit farther upstream, just to make sure we're not just around the corner from it." There's nothing worse than setting up camp late in the day, or at night, in a really horrible spot, only to find in daylight that you've camped within shouting distance of where you were supposed to be.

"OK" was his brief reply as he flung the pack from his shoulders.

"If I don't find anything upstream, we're going to have to camp here, mate, on this slab. I know it doesn't look too appealing, but it's the only piece of open flat ground I've seen all day. I won't be long."

With that, I took off upstream, feeling oh so light without my pack. Bouncing across the rocks like a gazelle, concentrating on my feet, I rarely glanced more than a few meters ahead. Less than ten minutes later, I became aware of a splashing, trickling sound in the distance, like a waterfall. It grew louder and louder until, as I climbed out of a very narrow gully, overgrown from both sides, I found myself standing in the shadow of a huge rock wall, a 30- to 40-meter (100- to 130-foot) vertical face.

"Jesus! Where the hell did that come from?" I asked, aloud. I'd been so concerned with my footwork that I hadn't seen it looming over me. It towered overhead, spreading completely across my path, almost 100 meters (330 feet) across. A ribbon of water flowed down the center of the face, a trickle rather than a waterfall, just enough to keep the moss growing. I began scouring for some kind of route, some trace of a potential way around, but this was the end of the road as far as the stream was concerned. The way both left and right led into dense scrub. Without the benefit of a gully to follow, I was soon forced back to the cliff base. It was too steep to climb, and, with the whole thing looking damp, it appeared totally impassable. This couldn't possibly be the way. The trail notes didn't mention any technical climbing. Besides, it was too late in the day to go higher, too late to be looking for another campsite while we had the slab to fall back on.

I made my way back to Geert to give him the bad news.

Rain

Head bowed, I shift my weight often, trying to get some relief from the steady, throbbing pain. It isn't the sharp, burning agony I first endured. Now it's like the deep, cold throbbing you get after hitting your thumb with a hammer. Every time I move to rearrange myself, which is often, Geert calls out again. "Are you OK, mate? Hang in there, you're going to be all right!"

Sleep is impossible for both of us. There is no way Geert can sleep, not with me in the situation I'm in. For me, the very concept is ridiculous. The rain continues coming down in bucketfuls while I try every position possible to get some relief from the discomfort in my legs. I feel like some kind of outcast, banished from the camp by an act of God. Only now can I appreciate how Geert must feel, huddled in his warm sleeping bag while I lie crumpled over the slab in the rain. He must feel utterly useless; I know I would. Every five to ten minutes he calls out, "Are you all right, Warren?"

"Yeah," I reply, above the din of the rain.

Well, I am, to the extent that either of us can be. It's almost as if I'm trying to put myself in a state of suspended animation, trying to blank out of existence the time between now and sunrise, not wanting to live it at all. I don't believe in willing the future toward me. Wishing time to pass faster than it already does is a sin I've been guilty of—but that's what it is, a sin. Ideally, we should all live for the moment, because that's the only certainty. Time is precious, and every second should be appreciated and enjoyed as if it's our last. That's my theory, anyway. I don't practise it completely myself, but I envy the few people I know who do. But now, with the rain and the cold and the fear, time can't pass quickly enough.

Is that an engine!?

"Geert! Plane!" The droning sound is unmistakable, even above the rain. The rush of adrenaline lifts me, as my eyes scan the sky for some kind of confirmation.

"Quick, mate! We need a fire!" Geert is out of his bag in an instant, scouring the sky for the source of the sound before scrambling off in search of something to burn.

"It's all soaking wet, Warren!"

"It doesn't matter, it'll burn!"—adding, as he frantically snatches up kindling, "There's a candle in my pack, in the front pocket. Use it under the small twigs, it'll take a while but it should get it going!" (Using a candle to light a fire is a skill I picked up in Tasmania, where it can be so wet, you almost need to be able to light a fire under water.) Geert gets it together quickly for someone who hasn't used this method of fire lighting before, but the wet kindling is still spitting and hissing in objection as the low hum disappears into the night. It may not even have passed overhead; neither of us has seen any lights.

Geert perseveres for another five minutes or so, but it's a lost cause. On the one hand, I desperately want Geert to get the fire going, and to keep it alight just in case another plane flies over. But it's such a long shot. I'm gambling on the theory that, because fires are not allowed on the island, it will be noticed and read as a distress signal. But unless the plane's occupants are familiar with the area (and a pilot wouldn't be able to make out the island in the dark otherwise), even with the no-fires ban, our attempt at a signal will appear as nothing more than a campfire. *Is it worth having Geert up all night keeping one going when he is going to need all of his resources in the morning?*

Geert knows I'm clutching at straws, but he doesn't say anything. He makes his way back toward the shelter of the tarp as I slump back over the slab, both of our spirits dampened after a faint glimmer of hope.

The drumming of steady rain on the hood of my jacket is louder, forcing my mind away from thoughts of rescue to the stark reality rising around me. With my head in my hands, eyes squeezed tightly shut behind my palms, my mind races like a roulette wheel while I pray for the little silver ball not to stop where I know it will.

The water level is now above my waist.

The Deafening Roar

"Geert!"

"Are you all right, mate?" His reply is immediate.

"Mate, we've got to try again. I've got to get out!"

"Hang on!" he shouts back above the rain, stepping into the rapid flow and quickly splashing toward me.

"The river's coming up! I've got to get out!"

I've been sitting here, feeling it rise, not wanting to accept what is really happening until I can't stand it any more. The trickle down the buttress upstream sounds as though a dam has burst: a roaring torrent cascading out of the darkness. The fact that I can't see it makes it all the more terrifying. I half expect one huge wave to surge forward and completely engulf me. That would make it a lot easier. Instead, I'm sitting right in the middle of its path, trapped, as it slowly rises.

I'm going to drown!

Geert looks scared. "What the hell do you want me to do, Warren?"

"We've got to try again," I gasp, almost pleading. "I can't stay under here, I'm finished if I don't get out!" Reaching under the shelf, I try to position the pillar of stones so they're standing more squarely on top of each other.

"I need more rocks, mate, not so round," and Geert's off, splashing in the knee-deep water to see what he can find. My hands are freezing as I work under water, trying to pull off the balancing act required. Fear keeps rising in my throat. I'm doing everything in my power to stop myself from just crying out and howling . . . from falling into a sobbing heap and giving up. *No! I can't die like this!* I shudder, then feel my own anger at myself for almost giving in. *I have to stay in control!*

Regardless of what one believes about drowning, whether or not it's the peaceful death some claim it to be, the position I'm in is more terrifying than anything I've ever imagined, though I've been faced with the possibility of drowning before, while snorkelling. That time, a surging current held me beneath a ledge I'd swum under to investigate, trapping me for what seemed like minutes before I struggled free, kicking and clawing my way to the surface. But that was all over in less than a minute. *I could be here like this for hours before the water slowly rises above my head.*

As if I'm not cold enough already, the thought chills me to the bone. My head fills with vivid images of water coursing around my face as I crane my neck to get clear. *What will happen? Will I just hold my breath until I pass out, or will I be gulping in water, trying to breathe but choking, gasping in water and retching again until I just seize up and die?*

Geert returns with more rocks, piling them up in front of me to form a dam. "It's all right, mate, I don't think it will come up much higher," he assures me, but I'm looking at the bank.

Why not? It has before. I can see by the light of the flashlight the telltale signs indicating previous water levels, and it doesn't look good. *The marks are above my head!* My thoughts are spinning. *What's the frame of my pack made of?* My last one had aluminium tubing, but I don't think this one does. If I can just find a piece of tubing, I could use it like a straw to breathe air from the surface when I go under. But how long will I last doing that? I'm already freezing. Geert's still piling up the stones while I smash away at the wedge stone. It's under the water and I can't strike with full force. Eventually, through exhaustion, I have to stop. Geert does the same. My situation is now so desperate, the only way I can deal with it is to accept it, slumped over the slab in submission. I'm stuffed.

So this is it, hey—this is how the story ends? Although Geert's right beside me, I'm no longer strongly aware of his presence. Withdrawing into myself, having given up any hope of survival, I begin to see myself as a character in some kind of bizarre movie—almost like I am watching myself from afar. *Will I get to watch myself die like this?*

Am I imagining things or has the rain eased off? It has! Geert senses it also, coming back to life with me. *Is this a reprieve?* Or is it just a prelude to the next stage, the next twist that even the most ardent art-house movie fan would have trouble watching? Geert's rubbing my shoulders in encouragement.

"It's stopping, mate. The rain is stopping."

I'm having trouble sharing his enthusiasm, not yet willing to venture back into a world that's turned upside down on me. I just want to cry with relief, but I can't. That would mean accepting that everything out there is all right, and it isn't. I feel much safer inside, preferring to peek out from under my dripping, but now silent, hood.

It is true. The rain has stopped. *But will that stop the river rising? We're very close to the summit, so the response should be fairly quick. Or is that just wishful thinking?*

Water is still roaring over the wall upstream, but it doesn't seem so formidable without the rain as a backdrop. As my anxiety gradually recedes, the throbbing pain returns to the forefront of my thoughts. *My legs! My legs are killing me!*

Geert comforts me as I rock back and forth, trying to tense my legs to gain relief. "You're going to be all right, Warren. You're a tough bastard. You're gonna make it."

I nod in agreement, "I know. I have to."

We agree to have one more try first thing in the morning, as soon as it gets light. If that doesn't work, Geert will walk out for help. As he leaves me again, I sense his reluctance to do so, but he has no choice. He has to get some rest, and there can only be a few more hours of darkness left. I watch him cross to the promised land once more, then turn my attention back to blocking out the pain, trying hard not to think about the hours that lie ahead before daylight.

I've seen quite a few sunrises in my time, but this must be the longest in the history of the planet. I watch as the sky begins to lighten to the east, so agonizingly slowly that, at times, it seems like nothing is happening, as if time has come to a standstill—that on this day, of all days, the sun will not rise. Then, ever so slowly, the sky begins to spread its glow, silhouettes become three-dimensional objects. *How long should I wait before yelling out to Geert?* I don't have to wait long for the answer. I am relieved to hear movement as he climbs out of his bag.

"Are you OK, mate?" he calls.

"Yeah, I'm all right." Which is far from true, but, considering the circumstances, I suppose I am. "Are you ready to go again, mate?" I add, knowing that time is critical now, and we have time for only one attempt before Geert has to leave. Otherwise he risks running out of daylight, and that will be the end of me.

This has to work, I plead to myself. All I can think about is getting out. I force the other outcome from my mind, not even wanting to contemplate it. Geert heaves on the sapling lever while I use a hammer stone and wedge. *Even if we can lift it a fraction at a time* . . . For half an hour we battle on, refusing to give up. As Geert pulls down on the lever with all his might, I drive the wedge in frantically. I am desperate to gain even the slightest reprise from the crushing weight, but nothing moves. I realize now that, when we moved it last night, we just helped it settle in to its final resting place. It is painfully obvious what has to happen.

"Mate, you've got to make it out"—almost begging him, feeling the acid rise in my throat, hearing the fear in my voice.

Geert nods, "Don't you worry. I'm going to get you out of here."

He sets about packing up: first his gear, then mine. He collects items that he thinks I am going to need while he's gone. In three separate plastic bags, he gives me a flashlight, my first-aid kit, half a loaf of rye bread, a small bag of dried fruit and nuts, a piece of sweaty cheese, a plastic mug, a blue polyurethane tarp, and my diary with a pen. He ties all three bags together with a piece of cord then slings that over my head, resting the bags on the rock in front of me like a fold-down tray in an airplane. The cord around my neck will stop the bags being washed away if I fall asleep or the river rises up over the rock.

Saying goodbye to Geert is one of the strangest and scariest things I've ever done. I do everything but beg him to be careful, insisting that it doesn't matter how long it takes him, he just has to make it.

"Stay in the bush alongside the creek if you can. It will be way too slippery in amongst the rocks, and if you slip we could both be goners." I hold back from stressing my concerns too strongly for fear of making him freak out any more than he already must be. I don't want to put him under any more pressure. But I am terrified. We both know how hard he found the hike yesterday, but neither of us mentions it. He has to go with my confidence in him, as well as his own in himself.

We go through the plan again. He will build a fire on the beach as soon as he arrives. If there are enough people at the camp, and they have the experience, he will send them up to me.

I take his hand, then hug him tightly, fighting back the tears. "I reckon I can last tonight, mate. But," my voice straining, almost breaking up, "I don't know if I can make it through another one."

With that, he stands, lifts his pack and slings it over one shoulder, then feeds the other arm through. It feels like I am watching him in slow motion as he adjusts his load and faces me one more time.

"Take it easy, mate, you can do it," I say as I grip his hand, then let go.

"I'll see you soon, Warren," he replies, before turning and taking the first steps of his journey. We have known each other for only a few days, but I feel lonelier than I've ever felt before as I watch him walk away.

GEERT VAN KEULEN: *Planning the Trip*

After I completed the Overland trek and the even more magnificent Southwest Coast trek in Tasmania, I flew north over a lot of good Australian hiking areas, a very satisfied and relaxed man.

In Tasmania I had been able to fulfill the main purpose of my vacation to Australia: to hike for about a month in spectacular wilderness, unwinding—without the big crowds—from the stresses that I had brought with me from Europe; and to get my head screwed back on properly—a spiritual refuelling. Two treks in windswept and rainy conditions had not only strengthened me physically and caused me to lose 7 kilograms (15 pounds) in weight, they had improved my mental health a great deal. I experienced many adventures, filled two sketchbooks with watercolors and one notebook with text, and ended up with a damaged camera—dropped in the Southern Ocean while I was photographing bull kelp on the first day.

My next destination was Townsville, where I intended to stay one month with Rohan Bastin, a very good friend who teaches at James Cook University. When I was back in Holland, planning my Australian trip, he had told me about a spectacular hike on Hinchinbrook Island, a protected tropical isle off the east coast of Australia, between the towns of Townsville and Cairns, close to the Great Barrier Reef.

With Rohan's minimal but enticing background information in mind, I had chatted to a few hikers from Queensland when we shared a campsite on the Tasmanian coast, eager to learn more about Hinchinbrook. That was the day before I crossed the notorious Ironbounds, a mountain range that can be dangerous as the weather there is very unpredictable. In the cold Tasmanian evening, these Queenslanders had told me what my proposed hike in the tropics would be like, about the challenging trek to the summit of Mount Bowen and the spectacular scenery that I would be rewarded with at the top—looking out over the Pacific, the Hinchinbrook Channel, and the mainland. Not a bad prospect.

In Townsville I paid $300 to have the camera repaired. In the second week, I visited the National Parks office and asked a ranger on duty what I could expect in climbing Mount Bowen: what kind of wildlife I would come across, what kind of vegetation, would it be all right to camp up there, and would there be enough drinking water? As we chatted, comparing hiking experiences, he advised that it would be all right to go alone, even though the guidelines require a minimum party of three trekkers. He judged my experiences in southwest Tasmania sound, and supplied me with a one-week trekking permit. I could do the trek in three or four days but I intended to take my time. He also gave me photocopies of trail notes written by other hikers (which he said he wasn't supposed to do).

With the permit and notes in my wallet, I descended on the biggest supermarket I could find and bought a pile of good food—much more deluxe than the muesli and instant mashed potatoes I had eaten in Tassie. I then said goodbye to Rohan and Trish, and hit the road on a Greyhound bus, which took me to Cardwell, the departure point for the boat trip to the island.

Diary: Cardwell, Sunday, April 6, 1997 I believe that Queensland is much more conservative than Tasmania. At least most of the Tasmanians understand that they walk on precious soil these days. Here, the emphasis is on development; nature lovers and environmentalists are not welcome. Cardwell is a town where a developer is building a marina. He has already damaged two Barrier Reef islands with his projects, and now another is in the cards. Although Hinchinbrook Island is well protected as a world heritage site, world-famous Hinchinbrook Channel, which separates the island from the mainland, is not. But because no construction is allowed on the island, Mr. Developer is going to build his resort right opposite on the beaches of the channel. Its precious marine life—the dugongs, tortoises, fish and micromarine organisms—will be forever chased away by the resort's powerboats, jet skis, and other smelly, noisy toys, and the island will thus be damaged little by little.

When the big bus rolled into town, we were welcomed by huge signs declaring Cardwell to be the best place on earth and others announcing "YES MARINA, YES JOBS, YES RESORT." Almost every small business had a sign in its front yard.

Sitting on the floor of the jetty, waiting for the ferry, I casually leaned against my pack in the early warmth of the day. Looking out over the beautiful channel, I thought about the area's unfortunate environmental issues.

IT WAS A SHORT but lovely trip. Dugongs and tortoises came up for air all around us, while shiny fish called "long toms" skittered over the water. The boat found a channel in the dense mangrove forests and took us to a small jetty, where a boardwalk led through the mangroves with its mud crabs to more solid ground. I strolled away from the other two trekkers and onto the beach, where I found tiny fossilized crayfish at the flood line. I sketched the scenery, which was a lot different to the drama of Tassie: the same blue skies with a long white sandy beach, but uninterrupted by rocks and instead edged with palm trees and tropical vegetation.

This was to be a slow, hippie style trek for me. And I had a couple of fantastic days and nights, swimming in the nude, walking alone on the beach, feasting on exciting meals, reading a few good books on meditation. I painted my watercolors with quite a different palette than I'd used on Tasmania, and in the comfortable warmth they dried a lot quicker too. I thought of the experiences in my hectic job that had nearly driven me crazy, and what I was going to do about that when I returned home. Being away from it all allowed me to reorganize myself mentally. It gave me quite a different perspective on things.

Diary: Nina Bay, Monday, April 7, 1997 Mosquito coils slowly burn in the sand around me, leaving circles of ash on the ground. Above my head the Southern Cross is suspended in an indigo sky, surrounded by millions of stars. My tent has not been aired for a week, so I've left its two entrances open to the warm evening air. I am relaxed and feel great. The first couple of days in Queensland were a bit hectic—getting used to the significant difference in temperature and talking so much with my friends. But now I'm on the beach of a tropical, unpopulated island—no mud, button grass, leeches, or frost. Coming to Australia and hiking in Tassie was an excellent idea. The hikes took the pressures away and a week on Hinchinbrook Island will lift the last of them.

ON MY THIRD island afternoon, I arrived at Little Ramsay Bay campsite, from which the trail leads up to Mount Bowen. Later, two hikers walked into camp, an Englishman and an Australian. We ate our meals together, sitting around the metal rat-proof storage box—apart from the jetty, the only "facilities" on the island. I'd heard that the bush rats keep an eye on hikers and go after their food and garbage. So after dinner, I dug a deep hole in the sand to bury my leftover pasta. (But that didn't stop them. When I woke in the morning it had disappeared.) I then suggested that the three of us go up the mountain. The Englishman decided that walking the route to the other end of the island had provided him with enough of a challenge, and he quickly said, "No." The other fellow decided to think about it. He borrowed my trail notes, then came to my tent a few hours later and agreed to join me the following morning. His name was Warren Macdonald. He was thiry-two years old and from Melbourne. We went over the trail notes and Warren told me he was an experienced guide who took environmentalists over "non-existing" trails in the Tasmanian wilderness. Deep in the rain forest, they had held up logging in the northwest—the Tarkine—while trying to focus media attention on the building of a road through this special place. Warren was immensely fit and strong and seemed to be a perfect partner. Most important, he was blessed with a good sense of humor, the icing on the cake. According to the trail notes our trip should take six to seven hours.

Diary: Little Ramsay Bay, Tuesday, April 8, 1997 The weather this evening is excellent, and I've taken the fly off the tent. Candles create a warm and cozy atmosphere inside, and lying on my Therm-a-rest I listen to the water washing against the shore until it takes me into a fine sleep.

THE FOLLOWING MORNING, we packed up our beach camp at 7:30 AM. I left my tent and a lot of other heavy stuff, including food, behind in the storage box. There was a logbook in there, and I wrote down our destination and plans. I was going to take just the essentials needed for a few days: plenty of food, a burner, rain gear, my sketchbook and notebook, plus a lot of enthusiasm and a healthy dose of curiosity. I put black-and-white film in the camera; I was on the prowl for challenging photography. Warren also packed his gear, including his tarpaulin; since we were in the tropics, we didn't need a tent. Happy to leave a lot of weight behind, we then started our trek, wading through a lagoon to Warrawilla Creek. There was no trail as such. A poorly marked path led to Mount Bowen over rocks in the creek. Hard going! Rock-hopping, cursing at the enormous stones I had to conquer, I went up. It was a difficult hike over very rough terrain as we wound our way, now left, now right, seeking the easiest possible route over the boulders and rocks.

My month of hiking in Tassie seemed like one day, compared with the level of fitness that Warren displayed. Christ, what a fit bastard. With his long legs he seemed to walk like he was simply going up a stairway instead of a rock-loaded creek. Because he was taller than me, he also seemed to have more leverage, which meant he could walk a lot more comfortably. In this terrain, going for a gain in altitude of some 1,100 meters (3,600 feet) is a fair plod.

It was a humid day, at the end of the rainy season. Most of the time I walked alone: slipping and sliding, hurting myself a few times when I "missed" a rock. Some were covered in a kind of black moss, which cushioned and provided a bit of grip when dry, but when wet, the boulders were more treacherous and slippery than a slide covered in green soap. Many had been eroded into smooth round shapes: perfect, round boulders strewn across the creek, as if dropped from an airplane.

Once, thrown off balance by my badly skewed pack, I slipped and fell in a rock pool. Just able to keep my head dry, I was out of the water in seconds, throwing off my pack and the camera bag around my waist. The bag has a center compartment with my camera in it and two side-pouches for film, lens cleaner, batteries, a pocketknife, and a cigarette lighter. I quickly got out the camera, fearing another disaster like in Tasmania, but the water hadn't penetrated the bag. Lucky! Still, I decided to give the camera a good clean, and continued the climb only after I had stored it properly. The sun soon burned my naked shoulders and dried my pants.

In another careless moment, I fell hard. I had been watching Warren easily maneuver to the top of a big rounded rock. "Obviously, he is a much better technical climber than me," I grumbled under my panting as, supported by a healthy dose of Dutch swearing, I approached the rock via the same route. But my agility could not touch Warren's. My pack continued to slide all over the place. It had endured quite a hammering in Tasmania, and now the straps, clips, buckles, and zips were protesting against this latest uphill challenge. Just as I was applying all of my miserable rock climbing skills to get up that round, red bastard, using my hands and the sides of my walking boots to gain holds, it again shifted, flinging me sideways. I fell 1.5 meters (5 feet) and landed hard on all fours. That hurt, and I stayed put for a while in the shallow water of the creek, looking for bruises and broken bones. I looked to see if Warren had seen my fall, but he was not in sight. So I got up, cleaned my hands, and continued, sweating not only from the heat but also from fear, exertion, and embarrassment.

The hardest part of such hiking is that I couldn't build up momentum. A diesel like me wants to keep going. But that kind of work was too much stop-and-standing. After each rock, there was yet another one waiting; looking around, I continuously had to choose a new path. The deep rock pools, small waterfalls, and cascades forced me to zigzag upward, frequently switching from one side of the creek to the other. Mostly, all I saw on my "joyous" tropical walk were stones. But sometimes, coming around the umpteenth bend, I saw Warren's head popping up above a little rock: a round object that grew as I approached, a red goat beard on the bottom of it, followed by a strong neck that rested on massive shoulders.

Diary: Warren has to be patient with me. I don't like it much when I have to frequently wait for another person. Do I imagine that he is secretly laughing at me or am I being paranoid? I'm sure that the tiredness makes me think less than logically. Warren is too polite and patient to do that. When I reach him, we talk. He reckons we are about half an hour away from the top! Now that sounds better.

Diary: We have arrived at a magnificent rock pool, and thrown off our packs to jump into the ice-cold water. Faaaantastic! We stick our smelly heads and bodies under a waterfall and play like children, shouting and laughing into the dense bush around us. I take pictures of the creek and of us washing ourselves under the waterfall. Refreshed, I put my thermal Explorer socks over my red, tired feet, remembering when I bought them in Adelaide some 12 years ago, the best Australian product I have ever come across. My mother has repaired them once, but I've never had any blisters while walking in them. In fact, I've covered so many kilometers in these socks that I've grown fond of them—much to the annoyance of my girlfriend, who thinks I'm attached to an ever-growing pile of junk. Then I laced up my German boots, which haven't lasted 12 years. This is probably going to be their last trip. Like my pack, the Tasmanian conditions have given them a hard time.

AS WE CONTINUED our stroll up the creek, the temperature skyrocketed. Sweat was soon running down my face and drawing traces over my sunglasses. Not long after leaving our sublime rock pool, my clothes were soaked. I was exhausted; by 4 PM, the half-hour we thought we were from the top had passed some three hours before. The creek had many side creeks and we could have taken the wrong one, but that didn't worry us. Finally, glad to stop, we threw off our packs at a large flat stone that was perhaps 3 by 6 meters (10 by 20 feet). Bordered by scrub and the jungle on one side and about a meter (3 feet) above the creek, it gradually sloped down to the water. Warren judged it to be a

fine spot for an emergency bivouac in case we didn't feel like going farther. I couldn't have agreed more and planted my bum on the stone,
where I rubbed tired calves and massaged a sore right knee. Judging by
our own walking experiences and the time of the day, we should have
been on the top of Mount Bowen by then.

While I rested, Warren hiked up a bit farther to check out the area.
When he came back, we decided to put up camp and head back down
in the morning. We couldn't afford more time on our trekking permits.
Mount Bowen would have to wait to be visited by either of us again.

Warren took his tarpaulin out of his pack and made us a comfy
camp, our Therm-a-rests providing excellent comfort against the hard
rock. While Warren attached the lines of the tarp to the trees, I cooked
tortellini, and soon the aroma of our cooking pot was mixed with the
scent of the rain forest, beneath the dark sky. Cooking after a hard day
of hiking makes for fine moments; eating comes a close second. The
tortellini wasn't good by a long shot, but we threw a layer of melted
cheddar on top of it, added chillies, garlic, and a few slices of salami,
and devoured it with pleasure. Anything would have tasted fine.

As we ate, Warren explained how he'd once worked as a wilderness
guide in Tassie. Quite incredible. He described, in fine detail, a friend
who had had a leech stuck out of his eye on one trip, and how his mates
all panicked. The lone woman in their group of tough men was the only
one with the guts to remove the sucker. Tales like that, quietly told,
drifted into the tropical evening. It's great to be here, I thought, re-
counting past adventures. A bond was developing between this strong
character from Melbourne and myself. Although I had only met him
the day before, it seemed like I had known him for a very long time.

It was a fine night, but by about eight, after the hard work of the
day, I felt bushed. I went for a pee, balancing on the edge of the slab
close to where the rock and the creek dropped sharply, a meter or so
from our tarp; it wasn't possible to walk away from our camp, and I
certainly didn't fancy more rock hopping just to relieve myself. I took
my boots off and organized my stuff a little. I didn't have the energy to
draw, but I took a few photos using the flash. Then, sitting on a rock,

I slowly cleaned my teeth, looking up at the black sky where the clouds allowed only a few stars to shine through.

"I'm going to hit the sack, mate," I said, using my best Australian accent, and crawled under the tarp.

AFTER CHECKING if everything was in place, I tied Warren's flashlight by its cord to the central tent pole, which carried the tarpaulin. My fleece jacket functioned as an excellent pillow, and I put my arms under my head, closed my eyes, and started to daydream, reflecting on the evening and the day. I was never happier: tired, but relaxed and content. While Warren was going about, doing his thing, I started to drift off.

Lying on my back, the first dreams were starting to come when, all of a sudden, I was woken by an agonizing yell from near the creek.

"A flashlight, quick. Oh fuck, get a flashlight! *Get a flashlight!*"

I sat straight up in my sleeping bag, not sure what was going on, trying to get the flashlight loose from the bar of the tarpaulin. I finally succeeded—in what seemed like an hour but was only a few seconds—and went outside and found Warren lying in the creek, covered by a big slab of rock.

The shock was enormous. Then the absurd reality of the situation hit me. I was dressed in my underpants and standing next to Warren, where he was trapped under the rock. Both of us were barefoot. It was very dark. With Warren's flashlight I checked his position, quickly scanning the area around him. It didn't look good. The rock was gray colored, shaped in a wedge, and had come loose from another, much larger, mother rock. Warren's left leg was completely covered by it, but his right leg was visible from the knee down. The knee seemed to swell by the minute. The boulder had trapped him very badly. What if it had covered him even more, damaging his ribcage, or what if it had only damaged the lower part of his body? All kinds of thoughts flashed through my mind.

Warren had been climbing out of the gully, to urinate away from the creek, when the rock—eroded over thousands of years—rolled loose and came down, Warren half under it. Just above his right knee, a sharp fraction of the rock covered his lower thigh; a small part of his upper thigh reappeared before the rest of the boulder buried the thigh up to his waist. His pelvis was also covered. With his behind he sat just inside a shallow section of the creek. About 1 meter (3 feet) to his left, the creek dropped several meters. Some water streamed behind Warren's back and fell into the depth. There wasn't much water in it. He was also sitting with the middle of his lower body on a small but tough tree. It must have just sat in between his buttocks and spread out from behind him.

The seriousness of the situation was obvious. Thank God there was no panic. Warren's calmness helped a great deal. What would have happened if he had started to scream and yell? But he didn't. And that allowed me to concentrate on the things that needed to be done: to try and get him out, to make him feel comfortable, and to consider how I would probably have to leave him behind to get help the next morning. The last thought, however, did not return in my mind until many hours had passed, when exhaustion and despair forced me to snap out of my focused, adrenaline high.

At first I tried to pull the rock away from him with my hands, but it wouldn't move a bit. I felt like I was tearing apart the tissues in my body. Then I started to collect wood: old and young trees with strong green limbs. Warren remained calm after his initial outcry, and we decided to try and lever him out from underneath the rock. The trees, young and old, would break and break.

AFTER THREE or four hours of non-stop work, I was sweating like a pig. Then it started to rain. All in all, while I levered the rock, Warren managed to pull himself out by only 10 centimeters (4 inches). Levering was particularly difficult because the ground behind Warren and the rock stepped up slightly. The rock had been broken by the fall in such a way that, instead of resting on his thighs and feet, it was crushing the length of his legs, falling in on itself like an upside-down bridge. Why hadn't it smashed apart in more places? Looking at the side of it answered my question. It was massive, probably 75 centimeters (29 inches) in places. The sides were very black and rough. It made me shiver. The large flat top was the part that had come out of the mother rock, and it was surprisingly smooth.

Meanwhile, the rain turned into a full-on tropical downpour. I draped Warren in his warm sleeping bag. Over this he wore his Gore-Tex raincoat (which would prove to be of priceless value). Every once in a while I felt so incredibly sad for him that I sat next to him on the ground in the rain, my arm around his shoulder, massaging his upper body and talking quietly to him.

The calmness that Warren displayed never ceased to amaze me. The man never seemed to panic. Sometimes I was so tired that I left him to sit under the tarp, desperate for some time to myself, to get my thoughts organized. On one of those breaks, my legs started to tremble and would not stop shaking until fifteen minutes had passed. I rolled a cigarette (thank God for tobacco) and tried to close my eyes for a few moments. Looking up again, I saw Warren's silhouette in the dark, his head tilted a bit to the right, rain smashing on his raincoat, and I think it was then that I heard him moan. That brought back the adrenaline, and the tiredness disappeared momentarily while I went back up the mountain to collect more wood.

There was no fear when I climbed up the green, forested walls of the small gorge we were in. Earlier, I had neatly stored my socks and orthotics next to my boots to dry them, but the water had washed them away. I was lucky to have held onto my boots, which I had to wear without socks, feeling unstable. While Warren sat in the dark in complete helplessness, I climbed, pocketknife at hand, the flashlight in my mouth shining through the wet green hell: too much grass, trees too thick. I climbed up the stem of a young eucalyptus and tried to bring it down by using my body weight. Hanging on the stem, somewhere above the creek, I hoped it would snap. But it wouldn't. I could only break it into very tough and annoying strips; the young, green wood had too much life in it. Of course! With the pocketknife I cut the strips. Soon my hands bled, though they didn't hurt. The handles of the knife had come loose. I longed for tools, a small axe or something, but we had nothing on us.

There was no time to worry about that, though. With renewed energy, we kept on trying to get the rock off. But again it didn't work. The water was also rising frighteningly high. Warren was scared of drowning, and when I looked up to follow the path of the creek upstream, I saw that what had been a small water drop—60 meters (200 feet) away, above us—was now a gigantic waterfall. I could see glimpses of its reflection during the night, and all that water was coming our way with thundering force. It was terrifying.

I SAT NEXT TO HIM again, as we tried to figure out another way to get him out. We didn't say much to each other. Each of us was aware of our race against time and the elements. Time was fast running out, and all of our efforts were to no avail. I needed to protect my strength; by doing so I would have the chance to save Warren when morning came. But I kept working against the odds, to curb my thoughts and sense of total desperation.

More tree branches had to be taken down. I needed more wood! Up I went again, crawling through the bush, flashlight in my mouth, and managed to get some branches down with which I once again tried to lever the rock. Sometimes I would actually get some leverage and, almost happy, both Warren and I would react with enthusiasm. It was possible to stick wood under the sharp point of the rock that was near his right knee, parallel with his leg and ending on the ground near his foot. A meter behind him, I'd then jump and sit with my body weight on the branch. While I worked the lever, Warren would use all his strength to pull himself out, his hands on the edge of the rock in front of him and a determined look on his face. He was literally peeling the skin off of his legs.

THE NIGHT ADVANCED extremely slowly. After five hours of near useless, energy-draining work, I needed a serious rest. I crawled into my sleeping bag, lay down, and closed my eyes, occasionally yelling out into the darkness to see if he was all right.

"How ya doing, Warren? Are you all right?"

"Yeah, mate. Yes," he would reply, and I would close my eyes again to get some rest. Never for long, however. Are you all right? What a stupid thing to ask! He was fighting for his life, and soon I would be back with him.

Around 4 AM, I realized I should prepare Warren and myself for the descent. We launched one final attempt to get him loose, mentally gathering our willpower and strength. But I had to give up early, as I was completely exhausted. The only way for him to stay alive, I thought, was to get a rescue party up there.

I knew what I had to do, and once again I sat next to Warren and discussed my plan. First, I made a small wall of stones to his right, to function as a kind of dam if the water kept rising. Behind his back, I made a sort of chair. All those broken pieces of wood could at least serve some useful function. I then stuck his Therm-a-rest between his back and the pile of wood of the chair. That way he was more comfortable and could allow himself to relax his back and shoulders during the long day and night ahead.

The rain had stopped at about 3 AM, and the water level in the creek was dropping quickly, as it always does in a mountain stream. By 5 AM, some sort of new life or spirit had come into me and I was under the tarp once more, preparing for the most important task in my life. In retrospect, that energy likely came from being able to do something useful at last, as I wrapped Warren's necessities and concentrated on how I was going to get down in one piece.

I found three plastic shopping bags in Warren's pack and filled one with food: muesli, dried fruits, an apple, avocado, bread and cheese, crackers, and a few granola bars. In the other bag I put some clothes: an extra shirt and a gray woolen vest, a few pairs of socks (which he could wear as gloves), a scarf to use as a bandana, and a cap for if it got hot again during the day. The third bag was for his diary and pen, insect repellent, and flashlight; his toothpaste and brush would keep him a little occupied also. A cord, which I removed from the tarp, I put through the bag handles then hung around his neck. The bags were positioned in front of him on the rock, which now functioned as a table. That way he couldn't lose them if another flash flood made things even more serious. He drank from a green mug, simply by scooping it into the water around him.

Earlier, before the rains began in earnest, I had wrapped his right foot in a plastic bag. But the water had washed it away and, later, when I examined the foot, I saw that all the color had left the flesh. It looked very bad.

I went back under the tarp to pack my own necessities. Many items had been lost in the rain, and I knew I was going to miss my orthotics—very important for steady feet on the hike down. Later I would find that I had also lost my water bottle and sunhat, as well as my socks, but such items were easily replaced. In that madness I didn't need them. I put on some of Warren's socks. And when I had packed everything, I went back out and sat next to him. I told him I was wearing his socks and why. That was the one time when I felt like crying, but I couldn't allow myself to get emotional. Not there. Warren's attitude was so impressive that we fed off each other emotionally. Because he stayed calm, I stayed calm, and vice versa.

SLOWLY THE FIRST light of April 10 appeared. I had planned to leave in those early moments at dawn, but decided to wait a little. The mist and gray atmosphere scared me. Then, at 6:30 AM, I repeated to Warren that the only way to get him out was for me to make it down in one piece and find help. He would have to prepare himself mentally for at least another day and night before there could be any chance of rescue. We were hoping there might be fishing boats in Little Ramsay Bay, as there were when we hiked up. I told him to keep writing in his diary and to try and meditate. I had been reading a lot recently about meditation, and I thought it might help him to not pass out or "lose it."

"Don't give up, Warren. Stay positive."

I was worried he would lose consciousness. I looked at his lean face and saw incredible fear there. His eyes sat deep in his forehead. It was a bald, pale face with frightened eyes—almost as black as coal.

"I rely on you, mate. Think about every step you make," he said. I replied that I was going to get him out.

"Tomorrow night, you're out of here."

To which he answered, "You're sounding pretty confident, mate." I told him I was confident, that I knew for certain I was going to get him out—that he, like me, must have read stories about people who had come through even worse circumstances.

"You are very tough and have to hang in there. Besides, I want to see your ugly face when you're back down in the world," I joked. With that kind of talk, we tried to ease our fears a little. Still, it wasn't time to leave yet. I sat next to him and we didn't speak for a few minutes. Before I could cross the physical boundary that was waiting for me I had to cross the mental threshold. Leaving somebody behind, helpless, and tackling the dangers of the descent seemed daunting tasks. But I had to get out and that reality made it easier. Also, knowing I would be in control of my own actions helped. Nothing was going to stop me before I reached the beach.

"Go well!"

I kissed Warren on the forehead, got up, and swung my pack over my shoulders. It was heavier than yesterday, with a soaking wet sleeping bag inside. I looked down to where I had to go and for a moment felt scared. In the daylight, I was peering down into a wild and angry waterfall bordered by dense bush: gray and green. There was no easy route visible, just water, wet slippery boulders, and rain forest. But somehow I would get down there, down to the beach.

I shook hands with Warren and took my first nervous steps. I slipped immediately, and heard Warren yell, "Go bush, mate. *Go bush.*"

My slip must have scared the living daylights out of him. His survival depended on my safe descent. I said I would, and then Warren spoke the last words I heard that day: "Go well! Go well!"

The Ultimate Test

In the moments following Geert's departure, I begin to confront what I now have to face, what I haven't wanted to think about while there was still some chance of avoiding it.

*This is it, mate, this is your ultimate test. This is the one you've been prepar-
ing yourself for all your life. I hope you've got your shit together. You better be good
enough, coz it's all up to you now.*

*Why did you come here? Why put yourself so far away from civilization? Is
this what you want? Is this a tough enough test for you?*

Should I even be here? Am I strong enough to be so far "out there" like this?

The questions surge through my head, threatening to crush me. I remember how, after one of my first wilderness hikes, Mom expressed
concern for my safety. "If I die out there, Mom, it means I wasn't good
enough," was my reply, much to her horror. "I'd rather die out there than
under some turkey's car in a supermarket car park!" But now, faced with
the harsh reality of such a possibility, is it true? *Am I ready to die like this,
out here, completely and utterly alone?*

Hot tears roll down my face. *Not yet, I'm not. No, I can't die like this.*
Geert is my only hope now. My life is in his hands. All I can do is hang on.

The rain has stopped now, and the early sun is spreading warmly
over my gully, heralding the beginning of another hot day. I feel like a
wounded animal, like those I've see in documentaries about Africa—
just sitting there waiting to be discovered and finished off. I manage to
eat a few pieces of dried fruit; I'm going to need energy. The water level,
still around my waist, is sapping the heat from my body. I'm constantly
adjusting the sleeping bag to counter cold spots. Knowing I'm going to
have to wait at least until the next morning is agonizing. The very
thought that, no matter what, I'm stuck here for another twenty-four
hours at least, hangs like a lead weight around my neck. Unable to
accept my fate, I feel so utterly useless.

What do you think you're doing just lying there? You've got to get out!

Picking up my stone wedge again, I place it in the gap between the
top of the pile of stones and the ceiling of the overhang, holding it with
my left hand, then belting it as hard as possible with the hammer stone
in my right—again and again. I keep going until I'm exhausted.

*C'mon you weak bastard! What the hell are you doing? Nobody else is going
to get you out of here. What if Geert doesn't make it back? Then what are you
gonna do?*

At that I start again, working frantically before falling back in a heap once more. Lying back, feeling like a total failure, my mind then takes the other side, playing devil's advocate.

What are you doing? Jesus, mate, take it easy! You've got to save your energy! Keep that up and you haven't got a chance!

I ride this roller coaster all day: busting my gut, then cursing myself for being so stupid. Finally, I accept the inevitable. I'm not going anywhere.

I know that my life is in Geert's hands, that he has to make it out; that I have no control over any aspect of that, that I can't make him go any faster. On the contrary, I want him to take it carefully, to be sure he makes it. My goal is just to hang on, to make sure I'm still alive when the rescue crew arrives. The thought that I might not be good enough to do that terrifies me.

—— SEEING THE LIGHT ——

Breathing hard, bent over with both hands on my trembling knees, looking down at feet that I could barely move, I'd rather have been elsewhere. I'd never felt so exhausted, so totally drained of energy. I felt like the other toy in the Energizer commercials, the one whose inferior batteries pack it in prematurely, leaving the Energizer-equipped guy to power on alone. That's who I was: the guy who couldn't hack it.

"Just leave me here, I'll go back down to the bus."

All I wanted to do was go home. At one point, I dropped to the ground as my legs gave way underneath me, my left calf trying to turn itself inside out. A feeling of utter uselessness filled me. *I can't do this. It's too hard!* But of course going home was out of the question. It was a team effort, a team-building character-building exercise. I was nineteen years old, in the third year of my four-year apprenticeship as a pipeline ranger with the Gas & Fuel Corporation of Victoria. Based in Ballarat, just over an hour west of Melbourne, my job was to carry out maintenance on the 120-kilometer (74-mile) gas pipeline between the two cities. Somebody had decided that, in order to communicate with the farmers whose land our high-pressure pipeline passed through, we needed to do a farming apprenticeship. So over three years, I spent one week of each month attending trade school at the Wangaratta College of TAFE, three hours north of Melbourne.

Now, don't get me wrong. I learnt some handy skills over those four years: how to de-horn cattle, for instance; how to knock up a quick mallee gate (a temporary gate in a wire fence); what to do when the sheep are all fly-blown or the Massey Ferguson just *will not* turn over. But Chris Truscott—who held the same position on the Gippsland pipeline, two hours east of Melbourne—and I were definitely the odd ones out. Our classmates were all sons of local farmers who'd sent their boys off to TAFE to get some kind of qualification behind them before they took over the family farm. And, finding it difficult to see any relevance between our jobs and shearing sheep, Chris and I were both fed up with the whole situation. So when I learned we would be going on a four-day hike into the Bogong high plains (in the state's alpine area), I looked at it as a kind of holiday away from the more mundane aspects of the course.

I soon realized that John Kirby, who organized the backcountry components of the course, was not your average teacher. I didn't see it at the time, but he tried to instill in us an understanding of the land—not just for farming purposes, but so we would have a sense of our connection to it. Above all, he wanted us to grasp our responsibility to it as farmers, who rely on the land for a living. And looking back, I'm sure he must have gone to great lengths to have that trip included as part of the curriculum, as it would have been seen by some of his peers (as it was to me at the time) as completely irrelevant.

A month before the hike, John suggested that it would be a good idea if we spent some time working on fitness.

Yeah, right. How hard can it be? We're only hiking; it's not as if we'll be running up there!

I went for a couple of easy 3- to 5-kilometer (2- to 3-mile) runs over the next month, nothing over the top. I was nineteen. All I wanted to do when I wasn't working was drink beer and have a good time.

"It would be better if you could find some decent hills to train on," was John's final suggestion. *Yeah, no problem,* I thought sarcastically, not realizing what I was in for.

On a Tuesday afternoon, we arrived at the trailhead campground at Mountain Creek, where we made camp for the night. We were all still treating the whole adventure as a bit of a joke, having no idea what could possibly lie ahead. I crawled out of the tent next morning into the high country mist wearing all the clothing I'd brought with me, including my woolen army pants. I hope it doesn't get too much colder, I thought to myself. And after a hurried breakfast, we were off, at a leisurely pace, along a dirt forestry track.

This isn't so bad. What was all the fuss about having to be fit? For this!?

We'd split into our own little groups, just cruising along talking trash, when John called out from behind, "ok, turn right where you are now!" I looked right to see a small track disappearing into the trees, but my attention was drawn skyward, as I tilted my head back to find the horizon.

"Shit!" was all I could say, my eyes following the trail as it snaked its way up the steep northern slope of Mount Bogong. Over the course of the next four or five hours, I would come to appreciate why the trail was called "The Staircase." My body almost begged me to stop every step of the way. The straps on my pack dug into my soft shoulders. Heart pounding, I halted every two to three minutes and leaned forward with my hands on my knees to gulp in huge lungfulls of air. I wanted to just take my pack off and lie down, dead, but John would have none of it.

"C'mon, we can't stop here. We've still got a lot of ground to cover. You'll find it much easier if you keep moving. We'll stop for a break up at the hut."

Bloody hell! What am I doing here? What does this have to do with my job?

I felt so weak, and I took my anger out on John, blaming him for my predicament. I started to hate him, and cursed him for getting us into this as part of our course. "I bet he's getting a real kick out of this," I thought, nurturing the idea that he'd already shown a dislike for Chris and myself over our lack of interest in other parts of the curriculum. But I wasn't the only one finding it hard. A couple of the others also wanted to go back.

"Nobody's going back! We're all in this together. There's no one back at the campsite. They're not picking us up until Friday at Falls Creek. It's as simple as that."

When it seemed like I couldn't possibly go any farther, I raised my head from my sunken shoulders to see, not just a very steep hill in front of me, but a looming horizon. Somehow, we had reached the top. But I was in too much pain, both physical and emotional, to take any pleasure in the view. All I could do was savor the fact that we weren't hiking uphill anymore. I had a quick glance around at the land lying far below. Then, before I had a chance to get my breath, we were off again. My feet screamed inside my desert boots. I'd thought they'd be OK for the trip. Now I was finding out the hard way that they were far from up to scratch, though the hiking was a bit more bearable with the main climb behind us. Still, I literally staggered into the Cleve Cole hut that afternoon.

Stepping gingerly around the camp, I felt ashamed of my weakness and avoided any conversation about the day's events. I felt like an outsider, that the others were worried I might hold up the trip and we'd be hiking well into the weekend. Everybody had complained during the course of the day, but I didn't think they were moaning about it as much as I was. I really felt like I was letting the side down, and was angry with myself for being unfit, so piss-weak.

The next day's hike, though not as steep, was not much easier. (The second day on any hike, I later learned, is usually harder than the first because the muscles that have been introduced to a new activity are now busy trying to recover.) I still felt like I'd been hit by a truck, but at least I didn't complain to the point of wanting to go home.

That night, instead of setting up in one camp as we had previously, John had something else in mind. Each of us was sent in a different direction from home base, at least a couple of hundred meters (660 feet) away, with a box of matches, flour, a water bottle, and the warmest clothes we had.

"Now, I don't want to see you guys again until morning. Make sure you follow your bearings if you leave your camp to get water, which I suggest you do. And don't cop out and go and visit someone else's camp. This is just for one night. I'm sure you'll be able to handle it."

As I lay next to my fire alone that night, I felt my strength begin to grow. I may not have been fit enough for the most challenging stretches of the hike, but I was relying on a skill that would serve me well in the future: the ability to keep myself together, to not panic when removed from the routine of everyday life. I knew that all I had to do was collect enough firewood to keep the fire going for the night and I'd be ok. I cooked myself a couple of rounds of damper (Australian bush bread), then fell asleep satisfied, with a full stomach—only to be woken by the dying fire. Feeding it back into life, I gazed up at the stars and for the first time imagined myself floating upward, trying to gain some perspective on my little camp on this mountain, what it must look like from above. Then, from further away, I zoomed up to see where the mountain fit into things in relation to the city far away—and where that city fit in, trying to comprehend my place on the earth itself. (*Try it. It's a grounding experience.*)

It felt so liberating to be outside under a blanket of stars, instead of cocooned safely inside a concrete suburban box. Although I felt vulnerable and exposed, I still felt so much stronger for being able to do it. *I don't need that roof over my head to feel safe and secure.* I felt safe and secure within myself, and that made my skin crawl with excitement. Filled with a sense of wonder at the powerful reality of it all, I was at peace with the world for the first time in my life.

I learned a lot about myself that night. I realized that I wasn't weak. Unfit, yes; but I could change that (and I did, as soon as I got back to the city, joining a gym and starting a fitness program, looking after myself more than I had been). What was important was that I'd begun the expansion of my comfort zone.

It was with great satisfaction that I walked back into camp the next morning. Some of the other guys hadn't lasted the night alone, and had returned to their tents before dawn. I couldn't understand why they could not go through with it. Was it because they couldn't stand their own company? Could they have been so afraid of the dark that they had to return to the safety of John's camp?

Of course, male bravado prevented any real explanations being offered; rather, what was put forward was, "My fire kept going out," or, "I ran out of water." I couldn't help wondering what they would have done if they had been in the same situation without the escape hatch: lain down and died? I felt a lot better about myself now, and about my part in the team—like I had proven myself. I began to appreciate our expedition from that point on. Some parts of the hike got harder, but I used the knowledge I gained that night—that I wasn't weak, that I could do anything—to push myself on. I even started to enjoy the challenges. At one point, high on a ridge, I looked back in amazement as John pointed to where we'd come from just that morning. It was so far away, I scarcely believed him.

I hiked out of the bush two days later very sore and extremely tired, but with such a sense of achievement. We'd covered about 40 kilometers (25 miles) over three days into a place relatively few people had been. Still, it wasn't until twelve months later, when I had the urge to do it all again, that I realized those few days had set me on a new course. For the first time I was aware that we are all stronger than we can possibly imagine, and that that strength is gained from pushing beyond what is known, what is comfortable.

Years later, while traveling across the U.S. in a beat-up Cadillac with four friends from Australia, I would come to understand this perception as a feeling of centrality—that we are in control of our own destiny, for which we take responsibility with every decision we make. My pal Dirk (a.k.a. Dirty) had just stepped onto a bus in downtown L.A., bound for the airport. He was flying home to Australia, just as Doug and Pete had done a few weeks before and Dave a month before them. That left me. Over the last three months, we had covered more than 10,000 kilometers (6,200 miles) in the Cadillac, which we had picked up for a song in Los Angeles. We'd been to Vegas, the Grand Canyon, south to New Orleans, then back up through Kentucky and the Black Hills of South Dakota before the car finally died outside Seattle in Washington State.

All of the other guys had taken time off work for this trip; except me. I had decided that there must be more to life than shuffling paperwork (after studying part-time, I had successfully transferred into the engineering department of our Melbourne office, trading overalls for a collar and tie). After being denied a leave of absence (which was devastating at the time, but I've been eternally grateful ever since), I threw in my career as a technical officer. It was the first time I'd tossed my cards into the air, and now, as I watched the bus drive away with Dirk on board, I felt an overwhelming sense of excitement. *This is it.* This is what I'd left home for. The last three months had been fun, but my real journey was only just beginning. Everything that happened now would be totally up to me. Every page in front of me was completely blank, and, rather than being scared by that notion, I'd never felt more alive.

Into the Black

In between bouts of restlessness, reaching into one of the bags for something to eat, I catch a glimpse of my diary. I've gone to pick it up a few times, but haven't been able to. To start writing will mean I've accepted defeat.

I'm getting out of here, I don't really need to write anything, do I?

I know why Geert put my diary in the bag. I didn't asked him to, and it's something we couldn't talk about. He would want it with him if he was in my position, and, though I didn't think of it myself, I'm glad he's left it.

I start writing, explaining what has happened; but I quickly feel an overwhelming sense of finality and have to stop. I feel I'm tempting fate by writing in the past tense, that it won't help me to stay positive. I put the diary away and hunch forward over the slab again—trying to numb my mind to take away the pain that keeps threatening to engulf me. All I can think about is Geert and how he's coping with the descent.

Please, Geert. You've got to get down.

My hearing seems to have become acute. The slightest sound of an aircraft has me reaching for the blue ground sheet. I use it both for protection (from the rain and the intense North Queensland sun that seems hell bent on frying me) and as a signal to any aircraft that may fly over. I reach for it at the slightest hum in the distance, stretching it out above my head when I think a plane is close enough to possibly notice me. I never actually see one, but that doesn't stop me pulling it out every time. *Please! Somebody fly over this way!* I'm desperate for a plane to see me, for a pilot to raise the alarm so I won't have to wait until Geert makes it out.

"God, he won't even be halfway down yet!" I think.

Lying back, utterly dejected, I contemplate my fate. *What's it going to be like to die? Will I die today? Is this how I'm going to die? Is it going to be painful? Can it possibly hurt any more than this or do you have to be in more pain before you die?*

I've never been this close to dying before, so how am I supposed to know what it feels like? Sure, like everyone else, I've lain in bed some nights, thinking about the concept of life. But then it just gets too much. I'll shudder at the intensity, my head shaking involuntarily at the incomprehensible concept of ceasing to exist, trying to dislodge the very thought from my mind. *What the hell are we doing here anyway? How can it all just finish? Will I still be conscious, actually existing on another plane? I'd like to think so but I doubt it. And yet, how can it possibly be otherwise . . . ?*

Have I even achieved anything while I've existed, or has mine been just another wasted life? Is there such a thing as a wasted life, or is every life intrinsically important? Sounds like wishful thinking to me. Haven't we, as humans, just elevated ourselves to our so-called high state of importance by putting ourselves above all other beings? Is there any merit in that? Aren't we all just animals, the same as the birds and the bees?

As I contemplate the terrifying possibility of coming to an end, my mind drifts back to another time and place, far, far away, where I had my first close encounter with my own mortality.

―― ZAIRE ――

June 1992 saw my arrival in Africa. After living in London and traveling throughout Europe for the previous two years, I yearned for some real adventure. Europe just didn't interest me any more. Sure, I'd had a good time there—probably too good. I'd hitchhiked my way across Germany numerous times (once right through to Turkey's northeast coast). I'd been at Berlin's Brandenburg Gate at midnight on the night of Germany's reunification, and witnessed east and west become one. I'd slept on the beach at Gallipoli, haunted by the tragedy that took place on the sand on which I lay. And I'd traveled around Ireland on a diet of soda bread and Guinness, sitting in ancient pubs as old men sang heart-wrenching songs about love and war. But Africa drew me to her like a moth to a flame. I wanted to see how the world used to be, wanted to experience it, be molded by it.

From the moment I arrived, stepping out of the terminal at Kenya's Nairobi airport, I sensed a difference—in the very air. Africa has a timelessness about it that is very difficult to explain. I felt as if I had arrived home, to a home I had never known yet had visited in my dreams. Then, after spending a month in Kenya and Tanzania, drifting from the savanna plains of the Serengeti to the island paradise of Kiwayu, it was time to get down to business.

My plan was to travel south through Zaire along the Congo River. I had heard that Zaire was a wild country, with danger and adventure lurking around every corner; that it was untamed and untameable. This was the Africa I wanted to see, not the colonial remnants left behind by the Europeans. I would travel on my own, preferring it that way because of the relative instability of the country. I didn't want to be responsible for anyone else if Zaire was as wild as rumor had it. Besides, the challenge of traveling alone in such a wild place was one of my main reasons for coming to Africa. Having a companion provides a buffer, and that was not what I craved. I wanted to be exposed to the raw experience.

Plans, however, being what they are, don't always run smoothly. I picked up a couple of nasty stomach bugs while hiking in the Ruwenzori Mountains, the fabled, mist-shrouded range that straddles the Ugandan-Zairean border. In a moment of carelessness, I assumed that the water gathering in small pools behind the Elena Hut would be safe. Perched precariously at 4,540 meters (14,900 feet), Elena Hut sits just below the glacier that crowns Margherita Peak on Mount Stanley. It is the tallest mountain in the Ruwenzori Range; hence, it doesn't receive many visitors. I felt I could be forgiven for assuming the water was clean, couldn't I? *Wrong.*

Struggling with a combination of amoebic dysentery and giardia, I decided not to throw myself straight into the perils of Zaire. It made more sense to rest awhile in Uganda, then to slowly make my way toward its southwestern border with Rwanda. My goal was to reach the Virunga Park du Nationale, just across the border, one of the last remaining habitats of the mountain gorilla. I wanted to see these animals in the wild, in their own environment, before they came to exist only in zoos. But when I arrived in Kisoro, the last Ugandan town before the border, I learned that civil war had again flared in Rwanda and the border had been closed. However, a couple of New Zealanders, Jim and Clare, assured me that the border on the other side of the country, the one shared with Tanzania, was still open. I decided to join them in a hitchhiking trip that would take us three days to get to a place less than 50 kilometers (31 miles) as the crow flies from our point of origin.

During one stage of this cross-country odyssey, I traveled in the back of a closed container three-quarters full with bananas while Jim and Clare rode in the truck's cab with the driver. Sharing my wooden box with two plantation workers, I bounced between the bananas and the container's ceiling as we careened down the potholed, poor excuse of a road. Two hours later, the smiling driver dropped us off and continued in another direction, leaving us waving goodbye at a dusty intersection in the middle of nowhere, and me covered in mashed banana.

It wasn't long before the next ride appeared. This time, I got to ride in the cab—along with six others. Crammed in like sardines, we made our way through the mountainous Rwandan countryside, our toothless driver grinning in embarrassment when he reached for low gear and Claire, who was straddling the gearstick, moaned her appreciation. It was good for a laugh, until he slowed to pick up another two guys hitching at the roadside. *Where on earth is he going to put them?*

Jim and I volunteered to ride shotgun, standing outside on the truck's wheel arches—raised a few eyebrows, it did, a couple of *mzungus*, or whites, riding like that. We must have got a few laughs from the locals.

Looking back, I know now that seeing the mountain gorillas of the Virungas has been one of the most magical experiences of my life. I was a visitor in their realm, an intruder, but at the same time I was aware of how responsible we humans are for the future of these great forest dwellers. The gorilla lives totally in tune with its environment, yet there we were, totally dependent on the equipment we had brought with us, visitors in every sense of the word. Today, the gorilla's survival depends on our finding a solution to the ever-increasing needs of the local farmers, who believe their only economic option is to push their cultivated lands farther into the forests, thus reducing the gorillas' domain. On top of that, the animals are hunted by poachers eager to make some money by selling them alive to zoos, or dead, in pieces.

It took us a full two hours to find the family of six or eight gorillas, as our guides hacked a path with their machetes through the almost impenetrable jungle. Once the animals' initial apprehension at our intrusion subsided, they went about their business, accepting our presence to the point of ignoring us. The wisdom in the eye of the silverback, the group's aged patriarch, brought a lump to my throat; his pride, his very presence, was overwhelming. I held so much respect for him and, at the same time, so much pity.

How could the future of such majestic beings be held in the hands of humans who have long ago lost their connection to the land? Did their demise begin when someone decided a gorilla's hand was the perfect ashtray for the office? Or did it begin centuries before, back when the Lord told us that the animals were there for us to use?

After a few days' rest in Kigali, Rwanda's capital, I began to feel strong again. Kigali, despite the mounting tension elsewhere in the country (Rwanda would later become the scene of one of the most brutal attempts at genocide the modern world has seen), is a cosmopolitan city due to the colonial influence of the French. A croissant or café au lait is never far away. I felt ready to begin my journey into Zaire. My mission was to make my way overland east of Lake Kivu, from Bukavu to the Zaire River, formerly the Congo. From there, I would travel downstream on the legendary floating village that plied the great river, taking two to three weeks to reach Lubambashi. It wasn't a journey to be taken lightly, and I agonized over the decision of whether to go or not. But believing my health was on the mend, I crossed the border into Zaire and walked the 4 or 5 kilometers (2 or 3 miles) of no-man's land between Gisenyi (Rwanda) and Goma (Zaire). No sooner had I crossed than I was struck down again with fever, and had to rest for another few days until my strength returned.

Finally, after a horrendously crowded ferry trip the length of magnificent Lake Kivu, I reached Bukavu. It would be my last taste of relative civilization before I headed into the dark heart of Africa, and I spent a few days there, just relaxing and investigating transport options inland. It took a couple of days to find a driver willing to take me to Kindu, a village 250 kilometers (155 miles) west, on the banks of the mighty Congo. Meanwhile, people tried to talk me out of the journey, shaking their heads in concern, saying, "Bad, very bad. Road no good" in broken Swahili.

I discovered quite early upon my arrival in Zaire that my limited Swahili was all but useless. Zaire is a French-speaking country and too far away from the east coast, where Swahili developed during the slave trade era, for Swahili to be widely spoken. Some people have a limited knowledge of it, but they are few and far between. Most people in eastern Zaire speak Lingala, a language I was having trouble picking up. My refusal to learn any French out of principle was now posing some drawbacks. (I have never forgiven the French for sinking the *Rainbow Warrior*, the Greenpeace ship, and for being so arrogant as to continue testing nuclear weapons in the Pacific—despite protests around the globe.)

Finally, I made arrangements to ride on a truck leaving at 7 AM the following morning, agreed on a price with the driver, then took to the market to pick up supplies. With trepidation, I lay in bed that night hoping everything would fall into place: that I had the departure time right, that the driver was leaving from the same place we spoke at yesterday. Things like that are easy to get wrong when making a plan with no common language. But there would be no problem over such minor details. Instead, the driver failed to tell me two far more important bits of information.

First, the road was passable by vehicle only for the first 150 kilometers (90 miles), as far as Kamituga, the remaining 100 kilometers (60 miles) would have to be traversed on foot. Normally, that wouldn't be a problem, but in the state I was in, I was having trouble walking a single kilometer. The second vital piece of missing information was that the area we would be traveling through was a "mineral zone," full of gold and precious gems—so precious that everybody passing through needed a permit. (Of course, I didn't find this out until the military police knocked on my door at 7 A M, after I arrived late the night before in Kamituga.)

I turned up at the agreed upon spot at 6 A M (an hour early, just in case), to be greeted by the scene of confusion that is mandatory on any African journey. The truck was surrounded by my fellow travelers, shouting and wildly gesticulating as they simultaneously tried to climb onto the vehicle, as if it were a lifeboat in shark-infested waters. At the same time, the crew were trying to load the cargo, including some twenty-five 20-liter (4-gallon) plastic drums. These were tied to the back of the truck, creating a bizarre, wedding-vehicle effect.

An hour later, I was still trying to get my legs through the entanglement of everyone else's when the truck lurched forward. We were off— thirty of us, jammed on top of an open truck, on top of the cargo; my white face standing out starkly in a sea of black. I soon learned that the only English speaker on board, apart from me, was Joseph, a school teacher on his way home to Kindu. Nobody paid me much notice; in fact, they seemed to resent me being there. Hoping that my stomach and bowels would stay under control, I settled uncomfortably into the tangle of limbs.

That first day, we covered about 100 kilometers on fairly decent roads, by Zairean standards, anyway, passing through the spectacular countryside, with its vast valleys of tropical rain forest. Huge rivers, with gangs of men working siftings on the banks, flowed through the valleys below us. The rivers had been diverted in places, by hand, by men searching for riches.

The truck had a crew of four young guys, whose sole purpose was to keep us moving; to keep the show on the road. They didn't do much for the first few hours, and I wondered why four of them were needed on board. Apart from loading the additional supplies we picked up along the way, their main pastime seemed to involve outdoing each other in giving me a hard time. They were tough bastards; they needed to be, to do their jobs. One wore a lone shoe, and constantly eyed my hiking boots. It fast became a joke, apparently, to give me grief over my every move. I couldn't understand a word they were saying, but it was pretty obvious: whenever we had to climb back into the truck after loading more supplies, which was often, they all hung about laughing at me as I climbed the side of the truck in my piss-weak state. I quickly began to hate them.

Night fell, and it was clear we weren't stopping. The stars remained hidden behind a cloak of black cloud, and it wasn't long after the first forks of lightning that rain began to fall. As we drove deeper into the forest, the road became increasingly overgrown; the passing of trucks like ours was the only thing stopping the road from being completely reclaimed by vegetation. When the first low-hanging branch swept across us, I laughed along with everybody else. But when the branches started to increase in size, I became concerned (along with everybody else). The yell of what I quickly presumed to be "Duck!" in Lingala became more and more prevalent, until we were all ducking under huge, sweeping branches every few seconds.

At first, I sat up with the thrill-seekers, eyes wide for the next branch to duck under. But as they kept coming thicker and faster, I spent less and less time upright, though because I was facing backward, I had to look over my shoulder to see when one was coming. Once, I lifted my head and was struck so hard that at first I wasn't sure whether my head was still on my shoulders or not. When my head finally stopped spinning, I was certain I'd broken my neck. One of those four young guys laughed. Hating him even more didn't help. Instead, I stayed hunched for the next couple of hours, my face pressed against my knees, not daring to look up. We finally reached a small village around midnight, where we all clambered out and headed off in different directions in search of food and shelter. After a quick meal, I found myself a place to stay for the night. Lying in bed in my mud-hut-cum-hotel, I couldn't help but wonder, What the hell am I doing here? *Mate, you're not strong enough to be doing this! You could die here and no one would ever know. Do you really need to be doing this? What the hell are you trying to prove?*

It was still dark when I was woken by the driver, and he wasn't happy. It seemed we had our wires crossed the night before when, I thought, he'd agreed to wake me in the morning. Well, he did wake me, I suppose—about two minutes before we needed to leave. Everyone else was already on the truck, ready to go. I frantically threw my gear into my pack, ran over to the vehicle, and heaved my pack up over the side. Climbing up, I was greeted with a tirade of abuse. Great, the sun was hardly even up and these guys were giving me hell already. I could imagine what they were saying: *What's wrong with you? You're holding us all up, you useless mzungu! Get your shit together!*

I was completely pissed off, and lost it quickly. I returned the tirade in English, well aware they couldn't understand a word, but knowing they'd get the message just the same as I was. I felt like the school idiot, the one everybody picks on just because they can get away with it. I didn't think things could possibly get any worse than the previous night's hell trip, but apparently they could. Indeed, they took another turn for the worse within minutes of our departure.

The state of the road was deteriorating (I wouldn't have imagined that that was possible if I hadn't seen and felt it for myself). It now resembled a cross-country motorcycle track rather than a road. In places, it was nothing more than a quagmire, with mud pits more than a meter deep that stretched for 30 or 40 meters (100 or 130 feet). We came upon the first of them within minutes of clearing town and immediately became bogged down in it. Everybody got out, and the four young guys went to work with shovels for the next hour, digging us out. The driver then revved the engine and released the clutch, spinning the wheels uselessly in the mud. After which, they unloaded the cargo to lessen the weight further. The rest of us began walking the first of many kilometers. Half an hour later, the truck caught up with us, engine roaring as the driver maintained his speed to keep the truck moving in the mud. He gunned it straight past us. After feeling a little apprehensive, I realized there was no need for alarm. With the state of the road, he wouldn't get far before having to be dug out again. I wouldn't have been surprised if we had to walk the whole way to Kindu.

When we finally did get back in the truck, I quickly wished we hadn't. The road cut into the side of a steep mountainside, suspending us hundreds of meters above the river below. Needing to keep our speed up to avoid being continuously trapped in the mud, the driver lurched the truck from side to side, as the left wheels, then the right, sank into the deep ruts. The deepest would topple us suddenly to one side, the truck balanced precariously, before we dropped down onto four wheels again. My stomach also dropped as I peered over the edge into the ravine below.

This is it. It's all over!

If the truck left the road on this stretch, there was no doubt we would all die. Sitting atop the truck, my legs entwined with everyone else's, I wouldn't be able to break free and jump if we started to roll. *How far will the truck have to fall before I consider jumping?* Then I realized I would have already jumped a dozen times if I could have—that's how certain I was that we were going to roll.

Sometimes, we tipped the other way, toward the embankment, slamming hard into its earthen wall, then scraping along it before we were thrown across to the outer edge once more. I was never so terrified, almost crying out in panic. I was certain I was going to die. I thought of all the people I would never see again, and whether my family would hear of my fate or have to suffer the uncertainty of having me listed as missing somewhere in Zaire. That happens in Zaire. If you're lucky, someone may hand your passport over to the relevant authorities and inform them of what happened, but only if you're lucky . . .

What the hell are you doing this for? It's not fair on everybody else, especially Mom. What are you trying to prove? I felt selfish for what I was doing for the first time in my life. Joseph tried to offer me some comfort, when I asked him anxiously if any trucks had actually gone over the side. "Many," he replied. "But only when God wishes it to be."

Not being the religious type, I found no comfort in his words. As far as I was concerned it was up to the driver to keep us all alive. There wasn't a single thing any of us passengers could do except hang on in white-knuckled terror and pray every time it seemed we would tip over the edge. I was never so scared in all my life. It took another day and a half for us to reach Kamituga. As if that wasn't enough, three days later, after being held in a prison lock-up for "trespassing in a declared mineral zone," in no condition to continue on foot, I boarded another truck for the return journey to Bukavu, back along the same road.

Alone

Leaning back into my Therm-a-rest, taking in everything around me (the rugged peaks, the whistling birds, the gentle breeze), I realize that, if this is to be my final resting place, I couldn't have picked a better one.

This is the way I've always said I'd like to go. Out in the bush, doing what I love. But is it? Totally alone? Haven't I already spent too much of my life alone? Do I have to die alone as well?

I think about all the people I love, especially those I wish I could have loved more—how I wish I'd told them how I really feel before now, before it was too late. I go through all my regrets, but at the end of the day decide that I've actually done a fair bit in my life. It is really only in love that I feel my life has been unfulfilled; it is the one thing that has always seemed to be missing.

I'm so thirsty, so very thirsty. It seems that I can't possibly drink enough. I continuously fill my cup by scooping it into the water that's still swirling around my hips. "Well, there's no shortage of water," I think, though the level has dropped. The fear of drowning has ebbed away with the water that was once up over my waist. The flow cascading over the buttress upstream has quelled. It's still coming over all right, but it's nothing like the thunderous torrent it was overnight.

The granite face that I hiked to yesterday—which seems like a lifetime ago now—is blocking my view of our intended destination, the summit of Mount Bowen. But I have a good view of "The Thumb" from where I sit—an impressive peak in itself, jutting, as the name suggests, like a giant thumbs up. Could it be the island's way of telling me, "You'll be all right, mate"? Or is it more along the lines of, "We've got you now mate, now you're finished"?

I begin to feel that, in one way, I'm now totally a "part of nature"— that, being trapped like this, I'm at her mercy, subject to all her realities, realities most of us escape from by existing in the protective bubble of society.

I think constantly about Geert, and of how he's doing on his journey downstream. *Has he made good enough time to have flagged down a boat at Little Ramsay Bay already? Is it possible they could be on their way to get me out right now?*

I have a nightmarish vision of Geert lying injured somewhere downstream.

No, he's gonna make it. He's got to.

The day seems to go on forever, time running in some kind of perverse slow motion. I long for the night, just to get it over with. The quicker it gets dark, the quicker it will get light again. I know also that it will be much easier to be seen at night, my trusty saber-light flashlight held under the blue poly tarp a highly visible beacon. In some ways, it will actually make a better signal than a fire, which could be interpreted as just another campfire. But a flashing blue beacon has to pose some kind of question for the beholder. So when night finally falls, I reach for the flashlight whenever I hear a sound, which is often. But I can't get used to my disappointment each time the hum of a distant engine fails to come closer and veers off in another direction.

God, I'm cold. So cold.

Rubbing my hands along both arms, I try to keep them warm. I constantly rearrange the sleeping bag around my waist, keeping it tight so the water doesn't flow straight through the fabric. The current drags it off me whenever I relax and loosen my grip, letting the water swirl around my unprotected body, sapping my heat and energy. Colder and colder I grow, thoughts of hypothermia filling my head. I'm increasingly afraid to go to sleep. "Go to sleep now and you won't wake up" is the warning echoing through my mind. But sleep still comes in short stints. My mind is playing tricks on me now. I wake at times in such a surreal state that I have trouble determining whether I've been awake or asleep.

GEERT VAN KEULEN: *The Descent*

The descent was ten times worse than the climb. An amazing amount of water was coming down, and there wasn't much of the area that I could recognize. It all looked the same. After a few steps, I lost visual contact with Warren; the noise of the water destroyed any chance to communicate verbally. But I yelled out one final time, "See you, Warren." I don't think he heard me.

I made it down the first slippery boulder. Thousands more to come. The fear disappeared, replaced by another burst of adrenaline, and slowly, unsteadily at first, I started down. My pack now functioned as a great tool, keeping me balanced. I also used it as a brake, the weight of the wet sleeping bag providing even more ballast. When I slipped, I would lean back and the pack would slow me down.

After an hour, I found Warren's walking boots (they had been washed downstream in the flood the night before) neatly stuck behind a few rocks, fitted together as a couple. I fished them out of the water, tied the shoelaces together, and placed them on a big boulder that was rising up out of a bend in the creek. If a rescue party came up, they wouldn't be able to overlook such a strong symbol. I also placed more cairns, but gave up on that after a while as it disturbed my concentration and momentum. Often, I had to maneuver very dangerously to place the stones on the tops of landmarks, and that led to unnecessary tiredness and fear. And fear was the most energy-draining obstacle.

Around 9 AM, all hell broke loose above me. Once again, the rainy season poured its afterbirth over me and over Warren in his trap. "Was this Mother Nature's revenge for our risky operation?" It rained so fiercely that I had to take off my glasses, which made me visually handicapped. I sat in the tall grass way above the creek for a while, the hood of my raincoat over my head, cleaning my specs and looking into the curtain of water. Carefully, I stored the glasses in my pack and continued down.

There was no time to stop for a long break. Sometimes I would slip off a rock and fall in the creek. I carefully stuck to the sides. Sitting on the edge of a rock, up to my thighs in the water, I would cup my hands and drink, letting the river ease my tired legs, then check my wristwatch for the time. I wore my plastic raincoat over a T-shirt, which made me sweat, so that I had to drink all the time. But walking without it would have meant that I had no protection against the thorns and sharp growth in the jungle. I preferred the first option.

Whenever the creek was too dangerous, I struggled through the bush, but that meant detouring around and through dense rain forest and the risk of ending up in the wrong place. That happened a few times. I would bush-bash through the trees only to find an even more dangerous situation farther in. Once I walked into a nest of green tree ants. The emerald-green insects, which smelled of lemon, quickly found their way under my raincoat and T-shirt, biting me all over. I had to throw off my pack and jump into a safe rock pool, where I frantically washed them off. The pain didn't last long, and I didn't get sick.

IT WAS LIKE hiking through a jungle filled with short, but tough, climbing plants with razor-blade leaves—like the milled edge of a gigantic steak knife. The grasses, many meters high, I held onto if I slipped while bushwhacking high above the banks of the creek, cutting the insides of my hands raw. I would kick the undergrowth, angry at it, then lose my balance and slide down when my feet lost all remaining grip. In one particularly frightening moment, I fell straight into the flooding creek. All I could think of as I slid over the rock into the whitewater was how not to break my ankles. I hurt my bum; my pack, shorts, and underpants had serious holes torn in them. But when I splashed into the water my feet found ground and I stood up to my groin. I was tired, angry with myself for losing my concentration and for taking the easiest way down. My heart was in my throat.

There were other moments when I would sit on a rock, checking my body and trying to ease the ever-pumping mental energy coursing through me. I talked loudly to myself to stay calm: "Quiet Geert, you have the time. Whether it's two, three, or four o'clock before you arrive at the beach, it doesn't matter." Every step I took I was confronted with Warren's purple socks, riding up my shins out of my rapidly deteriorating boots. There was a strong symbolism in that, I thought. Not only were they serving a purpose, they kept me thinking of my trapped friend. I planned to ask Warren, later, if I could keep them. Around my neck I wore a scarf my girlfriend had given me, and, deep inside my pack, I carried Warren's address book, wrapped in plastic. He had asked me to contact his father at the address written inside, and to give the book to him if Warren didn't make it.

Concentration was the key word for a safe descent, as, patiently, I made my way down. Yesterday, Warren had found an old red T-shirt somewhere in the creek and draped it across a big boulder—easy to see from either direction. When I saw it, I felt disappointed. I knew I still had a long way to go. Sometimes I lost my sense of direction. I had no idea how to judge the distance traveled, if I was getting closer to the beach. Sometimes I was afraid that I'd taken the wrong creek, but that was impossible.

There were plenty of young eucalyptuses, the same tough trees that I had tried to saw down the night before. In the descent they provided good strong holds as I bushwhacked down, even if they also housed the green tree ants. I *really* started to hate all the water around me and the branches that hit me in the face. In the Tassie wilderness I had laughed when some of the branches struck me. "Part of the bushwalking experience," I'd say to myself. But here they only added to the misery.

Together, the branches and plant climbers delayed me considerably. I tripped over them often, as the grass hid them. They loved to stick themselves in between the pack and my back, sometimes literally dragging me down to the ground—especially, it seemed, if I was too optimistic or covering ground too quickly. I was not allowed to go down fast! The piece of metal that had once been a proud Swiss Army knife now served as a jungle cutter for hacking the climbers' tendrils. At some point I lost my Therm-a-rest—bloody stupid of me. Warren and I had talked about how I should put it inside my pack, but I strapped it to the side, only to lose it. Another pitfall for the pigheaded hiker: imprudence is often punished in the wilderness. I must have walked past an impressive collection of native plants and wildlife, but I never noticed. All I saw was that the plants were very sharp and threw water over me when I touched them. This was no bird-watching jaunt.

The round, red blocks of granite made an impression also. During the ascent they had been gray and red, but the water and rain had changed their color to green-black, though "Warren's rock" was gray with white lichens on it. The creek was littered with round, smooth rocks, slippery beyond belief as they funneled the water that came from the sky and the mountainsides.

Sometimes I found myself in a situation where I felt decidedly unsafe. These were the most exhausting moments. I would sit down and try to peer closely at the landscape in front of me as a gray blanket of rain fell, blocking my view. Carefully, I'd check my position and look again at the rocks or, as an alternative, an escape route up through the banks. There were two choices only: dense rain forest or rocks and water. What to do? Man, what a scene. I'd wipe my hand across my face and feel the one-week-old beard, then try to steady my thoughts as I considered the possibilities.

Once, I let myself slide into the water up to my chest while holding onto some growth hanging down into the creek on the right-hand bank. Half a step at a time I shuffled through the mad water covered by white foam, balancing on my toes while I checked for drop-offs beneath me. The threat of a sprained or damaged ankle kept me very careful. I couldn't see the bottom and stepped on a few wobbly rocks, which made the blood curdle in my veins as I waded chest deep through what seemed like one long line of rock pools and waterfalls. I was also worried about getting a foot stuck under one of the rocks. But every time I felt myself panic, the thought of Warren, trapped, helped me to overcome the feeling. "No way, I'm gonna make it," I'd say to myself, and continue.

IN ADDITION to the dense undergrowth, the dangerously slick boulders, and numerous pools and waterfalls, I also had to cope with the noise. It was unbearable at times. Nature has created the perfect acoustic arena on Hinchinbrook Island. I have spent a lifetime avoiding noise: the clamor of supermarkets, traffic, stereos, and industry, to name but a few. In our modern society, I find silence is something we don't seem comfortable with any more. A bad development. But there, I was accompanied by a complete symphonic orchestra. I wondered if this was where composers got their inspiration. There would be a basic rhythm, which varied in tone with the terrain: sometimes quiet and only in the background, but often interrupted by angry soloists, wild trumpet play, and the remarkably accurate beat of a kettledrum; then a hissing sound as I shuffled through the creek; screaming, when I walked through the bush. It never stopped.

Sometimes I would be high above the creek, away from the worst of the noise, and would sit down. But the cacophony was always there. Yet it *was* useful. It kept me awake and on edge.

When I was lucky, I found a stretch of ground, perhaps 100 meters (330 feet) across or so, where nature had created some sort of pathway. I would come around one of the thousands of bends and there it would be: right in front of my eyes the foliage would open up, and there would be a long horizontal slab of rock that I could walk on with no interference from bushes or stones.

THE RAIN STOPPED around noon, and my tiredness came to the fore. The temperature quickly rose as the sun filtered through the clouds. So I sat down, ate a few granola bars, rolled a cigarette (I kept those dry no matter what happened), and dragged all the nicotine and heat into my body until I almost burned my lips. It was looking like I'd never get down. A few times I'd fallen hard and I was bleeding all over. Once again my legs started to shake, but I held them still by putting my hands on my knees. Slowly, however, I *was* making progress. At about 3 PM, I arrived in an area where there had been a bushfire. The undergrowth had been burned, and I was finally able to cover some ground quickly. It was here that I discovered where we had lost the trail, quite early the previous day, at some missed markers on the rocks and trees.

AT 4:30 PM I arrived at the lagoon. It had taken us eight and a half hours to hike up, eleven for me to get down. The last hour, knowing I was going to make it, made me enormously tired and I could hardly walk. But at the camp I found no one, to my disappointment. I would have liked to pass the torch on to another trekker, who could then hike back to the starting point of the trail. But there was nobody, and due to the storm there were no fishing boats in the bay, either.

Lethargically, I decided that it didn't matter. For the first time I doubted that Warren was going to make it. I felt depressed. I threw off my soaking wet pack, undressed, and walked to the ocean, where I washed my wounds with saltwater and examined my body. It looked pretty ugly. The bushwhacking had left its mark. My hands and fingers were completely cut open, and carefully, I put plasters and bandages around them. My eyelids were bleeding, my knees and legs slashed all over. I vomited in the sand. My glasses had received a few knocks as well. I took a little mirror out of my toilet bag and examined my face: one lens of the skewed frame of my glasses partially covered my eyebrows.

I hung my clothes, pack, sleeping bag, and walking boots to dry on the branches of the scrub edging the beach. The wind would take care of them. My shorts were ripped, underwear too; my boots were also fit for the dump, with big holes and tears at the seams. Warren's purple socks had holes in them.

With long, dried palm leaves, driftwood, and tree branches, I started a big fire. Warren, always thinking, had given me his whistle and an empty aluminum bag from a wine cask. He had told me to make a fire, then blow the whistle and wave with the bag to attract fishing boats—if they were there, of course, which they weren't. Dressed in my sarong I walked out onto the beach of Little Ramsay Bay and sat down in the sand. I looked up at Mount Bowen. The summit was obscured by white clouds. As I stared up at the sky around me, it was overcast, but nowhere as thickly as near the mountain. The foothills in the foreground were sporadically bright green but mostly dark olive in color. Where the hills ended, the cliffs of Bowen rose vertically—I judged Warren's position to be somewhere at the base of them, but I wasn't certain. I'd been in such a thick jungle and was too occupied with getting down in one piece to have a sense of perspective. There weren't any landmarks in my mind. Up there it was just green, noisy, and wet.

There was no point in walking to the starting point of the trail today. The tourist boats would not be coming in tonight. It was better to make camp and rest before hiking in the morning. So I set up my tent, which took me half an hour instead of the usual five minutes, and prepared another pasta meal, moving like a zombie. But I was too tired and too wound up about Warren to eat; I threw out the food and cleaned the saucepan in the sea. I also put a big SOS in the logbook, kept in the storage box. According to its pages, no one had passed through the camp yesterday or today. I crawled inside the tent and tried to sleep on the sand, covered by my sarong. The fire was still going on the beach. I had thrown a big pile of wood on it.

Dreams

The room is filled with a mass of seething, naked bodies, engaged in every sexual act imaginable. From amongst the throng a familiar face appears; a former lover who takes my hand and leads me out of the room. "Hey! What's wrong with this room?" I protest, as she leads me into another. Waiting for us on a huge bed is a different woman, unfamiliar to me. I sit down on a chair beside the bed as Leena crawls slowly across to her "friend." Sitting back in my seat, I watch transfixed as they begin, caressing and exploring each other's bodies. Just when I'm beginning to wonder whether I can remain a bystander any longer, Leena turns to me and smiles, beckoning me over with a single finger motion, as if to say, "C'mon, what are you waiting for? Isn't this what you always wanted?"

I step forward to join them, heart pounding as I squeeze myself between them. The three of us seem to mesh together, the heat from our bodies intense, almost burning. Our sweat mingling, we melt into one . . . then suddenly, we're alone, just Leena and I.

"Where . . ." I begin, only to be cut short by a finger to my lips.

"Shhhhhhh. It's OK. That's not all you wanted, is it?" she asks provocatively.

Before I can answer, she begins to take me on a journey through all the sexual fantasies I've entertained but never had the guts to partake in. Abruptly, and very reluctantly, I'm then snapped back to the present. Or am I? Drifting in and out of sleep, the boundaries are so blurred, I can no longer distinguish between dreams and reality. This makes my next dream all the more difficult to accept.

I'm involved with a group of Chinese businessmen, and these guys are incredible. They go about setting up business deals, trading in merchandise, shares, whatever, using the power of illusion to scam people in any - way they want—from showing prospective buyers through a building that doesn't exist to luring corporate executives into schemes that can't possibly work. They use the power of positive thinking in such a way that, when they think about something strongly enough, it becomes reality— and not only for themselves, but for those they choose to wield power over. No matter what the problem, these guys have an answer for it.

They teach me to use these skills too, within myself, and I become involved in some amazing scams, but, more important, I'm left thinking—no, knowing—that I can really be out from under this rock at any time. The reality of being trapped drifts into the dream intermittently, but it's not of great importance. All I have to do us think about it strongly enough, and I can be somewhere else. *I may not even be here, anyway; it could just be a figment of my imagination . . .*

So realistic is the dream that, when at first I find myself still trapped, I think it's just a case of me not doing it properly, of my not being skilled enough in the art of the mind. So I try again and again, unwilling to accept the truth until, finally, reality hits home. The dream was so real that I'm utterly devastated when I finally accept that it has been just that: a dream.

You're dreaming, mate. You're still here and you are not going anywhere. It didn't work. It was all bullshit!

I'm still here. How the hell can I still be here? How can it be true, I was so close?

Tears come freely as I cry myself back to sleep, shattered and disillusioned, freezing cold.

Good News, Bad News

The dreams are so real, they totally distort my concept of time. I wake to sunshine on Friday morning, but believe it's Saturday. It may have been the different time settings in the dreams or drifting in and out of sleep. Whatever the reason, the thought of today being Saturday completely devastates me.

Noooooooooooo! Why is this happening? What have I done to deserve this?

The *water!* The water's dropped right away. Only a trickle is flowing down the buttress upstream, a far cry from the flood it was less than twelve hours ago. The level in the creek around me has dropped so much, I wonder what I'll do if it drops any further. I'l have trouble filling my cup if it does. As it is, I now have to reach well out from my body to a pool deep enough to get a decent cupful from. *What if it dries up completely? No, don't even think about it.*

After drinking my first cup of water for the day, I notice a pressure in my bladder that reminds me of what I set out to do before becoming trapped, and I'm reminded of the fact that thirty-four hours have passed since then. Talk about holding on. I let my bladder relax and feel the hot flood of urine over my thighs. It doesn't even occur to me that I have to do it. I just do it, sitting there. It actually feels good, kind of liberating, to just sit there and let myself go. It's even better than pissing in a wetsuit. I can almost see the attraction for those who get their kicks out of so-called "water sports." *Almost.*

The feeling in my legs hasn't changed. I still feel like I can flex my left leg, even though I can't see it and have no idea as to the extent of the damage done. As for the right, I weep loudly upon noticing the green spots on my gray-looking foot. The knee is still very swollen, with dry, crusted blood around the gash just below the cap.

"*I'm going to lose that foot,*" I realize suddenly. The thought chills me.

No, they'll be able to save it, won't they? I can't lose it! God! What the hell's the other one like? Is it as bad?

I push the repercussions from my mind, knowing somehow that I have far more important things to focus my energy on, like my immediate survival.

Helicopter!

I grab the blue tarp quickly from my lap, and keep it ready for what seems like an eternity. *Am I imagining things?* It sounds closer this time, but still, it seems to be everywhere but here, near me.

Come on, I'm not over there for God's sake!

The hum fades into the distance and I let the tarp fall back into my lap. If this were a movie, no one would believe the cruelty of the script writer, how he or she can be teasing me like this.

Am I hallucinating? Are those vultures sitting up in those trees? They're probably just dead branches, but I don't recall seeing them yesterday. They're patiently waiting up there for me—ready to move in as I become too weak to fight them off.

Having run out of dried fruit late yesterday, I pull out the bread and cheese. I take a bite of the bread, a heavy German rye, and wince as it digs into my mouth, all dry and hard. It feels like sawdust, sticking to the roof of my mouth and the insides of my cheeks.

My saliva. I've got no saliva, that's what it is.

I fill my cup and, adding some water to the bread in my mouth, start chewing. It tastes awful, and my face involuntarily screws up in revulsion. My guts churn. It's not long before I'm overwhelmed by the urge to eject the contents of my stomach. Leaning to my left as far as possible, trying not to get any on me as I spew, I feel like a pathetic old drunk. Some runs down my chin onto my jacket. I groan, then retch again, and then again, this time bringing up nothing but yellow bile. *God I feel sick. I don't like this. This is not a good sign.*

I'm more lucid now, since I started vomiting, which is increasing my dehydration. During one of these retching spells (I've spewed up nothing more than the little water I've drunk; food just won't stay down), I notice a pool of blood spreading around my right foot. *What the hell is this? Why am I bleeding now? I can't start bleeding now. I would have started straight away, not now, not after all this time!*

I feel an icy lump in the pit of my stomach as I realize how helpless I am to deal with this. I can't even reach my foot from here, can't even twist it to get some idea of where the blood's coming from. All I can do is look at it and hope that it stops bleeding.

I'm still wondering about the cause of the bleeding, and what it might mean, when a movement under my foot catches my eye: the unmistakable form of a freshwater lobster (a "yabby" to an Australian). *A yabby! A yabby is chewing into my foot!*

"Piss off!" As I yell out, it ducks back into the red cloud. I can't feel anything. I don't know if it's still at my foot or what's happening.

"Mate, you're finished!"

Breaking a switch off one of the branches supporting my back, I take aim, ready to strike with my new spear. Hours seem to pass before he makes his next appearance. I drive the spear forward.

"Take that, you bastard!"

He's too quick, darting back under my foot as my spear hits the water above him. Half an hour later, he's back again. Again, he's too quick for me. *This is too bizarre.* I feel like I'm in a movie that keeps getting weirder. *This can't happen in real life!*

Feeling drowsy again, I worry about what he's going to do when I'm asleep. If he's caused me to bleed this much already, what's going to happen when my feet get softer? And they are only going to get softer. Will that mean he'll do enough damage to leave me bleeding to death, if he gets in deep enough?

The thought sickens me. *No way!* Taking off my green cotton shirt, I wrap it around the end of my stick, reach down and try to wrap it around my foot. The first couple of times I can't get it tight enough, and it needs to be tight. It's not going to work if it just obscures him from my view; before I can even contemplate relaxing, I've got to be fairly sure he can't get at my foot anymore.

The cold is affecting me more now. My left hand is turning numb, my little finger has curled involuntarily. I take this as a sign of increasing hypothermia. *They've got to get here soon. I can't last another night like this.*

Shouldn't Geert have made it by now? Surely someone would have noticed me not being at the other end for my ferry pickup? How long will they wait before raising the alarm? They may wait until tomorrow before sending a ranger to walk the trail, depending on reports from other hikers as to our whereabouts.

I can't imagine any search beginning before noon tomorrow. I don't think I'll be around by then, not the way things are going now. I can't even hold water down any more. I'm spewing it up and dry-retching for ages afterward. It really is starting to look like this is it.

It's all over—no doubt about it.

A Bad Movie Gets Worse

Just when it seems that things can't possibly get any worse, I feel a sting at the top of my right thigh, almost in the groin. *Shit, what was that?* Instinctively, I reach down quickly to rub the bite, then look for what's biting me. I can't believe what I see. For what I can see of me is covered with ants.

Bloody ants! Piss off, I don't need this!

There are lots of them. And they're biting me. As quickly as I can kill them they are replaced by others, just as angry. I carry on slapping at them whenever I'm bitten, which is becoming more and more frequent, until the absolute horror of what is happening becomes apparent. At the far end of my rock is a trail of ants, disappearing under the slab and marching toward me. They are actually forming a trail, and, obviously, swarming all over my legs, where I can't see them, as well as up onto my waist. From here, I can follow the column with my eyes back to the remains of an ant nest, which, until recently, was behind a slab of rock on the gorge wall—until I disturbed it, that is. Their nest has been destroyed and they've just found a new one with a ready food supply: *me!* *They're moving their nest over to me! No! This can't be happening.*

This isn't just any movie I've ended up in. This is one of those weird, art-house movies, like something David Lynch would conjur up. Horrific scenarios fill my mind, visions anyone who has ever come across a dead animal, covered with ants, is familiar with. The ants invade the body openings first, gnawing away in great numbers, eating the carcass via the ears and eyes. Then they eat out its insides, leaving at first just the skin frame, then only the clean, white bones . . .

Repellent! I've got some repellent in my first-aid kit, left over in a tube I picked up in Kenya. It should be toxic enough for them.

I've avoided using the repellent until now, highly suspicious of its active ingredients. But quickly unscrewing the cap, I rub it into the tops of my thighs as far down as I can get, then across into my groin as far as I can reach. *You're not getting in there you little bastards!*

Next, I rub it all through my hair, then around my ears. Finally, I rub it as close as I safely can around my eyes. *I hope this stuff works.*

I feel so cold and tired, but know I can't afford to sleep. I'm worried about becoming hypothermic. I have to stay awake. The repellent isn't really stopping the ants from biting my legs, though it does seem to be keeping them off my face. I haven't seen the yabby since getting distracted by the ants, and now the initial surge of adrenaline that accompanied those events has dissipated, I feel really, really tired. It's no use: I just can't keep my eyes open. Unable to resist any longer, I succumb and drift in and out of sleep, with dreams again so real they meld with reality.

I am floating, looking down at Geert talking to someone. He's in the ranger's office, relaying what's happened, that we need help urgently. I can see the ranger nodding his head, but he doesn't really believe Geert's story. "We'll sort it out, mate," he reassures Geert, then arranges a helicopter for a search. He flies the mission alone, making a halfhearted attempt at finding me. He doesn't believe I'm out here, but that Geert, with his Dutch accent, has got his wires crossed somehow. He doesn't fly anywhere near me and returns back to his office to get on with the more important task of paperwork.

Have I just been dreaming? Is that true? Did I really just see that? I've never really believed in out-of-body travel, but the experience is so real, I know I have to do something, to let him know it's true, that there is somebody out here. I consciously try to travel out of my body to get to the ranger. I see myself float above the treetops, across ridges and valleys, then into his office. I don't want to freak him out with my presence, so I put myself into his head, as if I'm speaking directly with his conscience.

"Mate, there's somebody out there. You've got to go and have another look. The guy wasn't kidding you—there really is somebody out there; just below the summit of Mount Bowen, trapped under a rock in Warrawilla Creek. Please go and have another look."

With that, I return, incredibly drained and satisfied that I've done my best, and open my eyes with the bizarre feeling of not knowing whether I've been dreaming or not. It all felt so real. Maybe I'm still dreaming. I just don't know anymore.

The day is drawing to a close. There is nothing else I can do but sit and wait for night to fall. I can feel the cold again. My left hand is totally clawed now, my right hand is numb. I try speaking, to see whether my speech is slurred (the next stage of hypothermia), but it sounds OK. I'm not reassured, though. I've all but given up. I'm really only waiting to die. The vultures are still watching me from the gum trees downstream, waiting . . .

So this is what it's like to die slowly, all alone, out in the bush. It doesn't feel as glamorous as I thought it would—maybe because it has taken so long.

My mind drifts back to another time and place, when I met someone who would be able to relate to how I feel now: someone who has stared death in the face.

―――― ROGER ――――

In the northwest corner of Tasmania is an area known as the Tarkine. It is a wild land, shaped to some degree by the wild weather it is subjected to. The coast is hammered by wind pushed across the Southern Ocean by the roaring forties, combined with massive ocean swells. Behind huge coastal sand dunes, button grass plains stretch inland 15 kilometers (9 miles) to the foothills of the Norfolk Range. Meandering rivulets carry the average 3 meters (10 feet) of annual rainfall through temperate rain forest, then tea-tree scrub, before depositing the now tannin-stained water into the ocean.

I first heard of the Tarkine while staying with friends in the north-eastern corner of Tasmania, friends I'd met in Germany four years earlier and had contacted again on my arrival in the state in February 1995. Christine and Ebihard (Ebi) Haas live in a small town called Weldborough, about two hours' drive east of Launceston. In the peace and tranquility of the Blue Tier and the Weld Valley, they were raising four children. Seppi, Carl, Eleanor, and Lara were learning from an early age to respect the environment, and were encouraged to entertain themselves in their incredible natural surroundings.

Ian Matthews, a good friend of Christine and Ebi, worked for the Wilderness Society, a non-profit organization dedicated to preserving the Australian wilderness. One night he told me of the tragedy that was occurring in the northwest; of how the Tasmanian government, against the advice of the federal environment minister, had begun construction of a road through the heart of the Tarkine. The Western Explorer, or Link Road, had been pushed ahead by a handful of politicians under the guise of completing a tourism loop in the state's northwest. Given the government's atrocious environmental record, it was fairly safe to assume that the access this road would provide to the massive stands of old-growth forest in the Tarkine's interior was of far greater interest than tourism. Cutting through the heart of the largest tract of temperate rain forest in the Southern Hemisphere, the road would also cross one of Tasmania's last wild rivers, the Donaldson. I'd been amazed, in my short time spent in the state, at the extent of logging operations—and I'm not talking about timber harvested from pine plantations. Huge trucks careened around the state carting loads of native timber, some of it from trees so huge that only two or three logs would fit on a single truck.

I couldn't believe my eyes driving toward Cradle Mountain, Tasmania's premier tourist destination, where a huge area of forest had been clear-felled right beside the road. What kind of a message was that to be giving people who come from all over the world to revel in what their own countries lost long ago? Nature. Wild, unspoilt nature. The Tasmanians have it, and look what they're doing to it.

Ian's insistence that this was Australia's biggest environmental battle since the 1982–83 Franklin River campaign (an environmental struggle that saw more than 1,400 people arrested, eventually forcing a change of government—such was the tide of public support) had me more than intrigued. I was already concerned about what we were doing to Australia's vast wilderness, how huge tracts of it were being developed and tamed—effectively, disappearing. I decided to go and have a look for myself, to see exactly what was happening in this "Tarkine."

From the moment I arrived, I was captivated. I had never been in rain forest like it: dark, primeval stands of trees, towering as they had for thousands of years. I sat quietly in places I'm sure had never seen another human being, where a sense of timelessness filled me. Unable to walk away from the destruction I was witnessing, I then joined the protesters. And over the ensuing months, we developed into a tight-knit group, labelled in the media the Tarkine Tigers. We established ourselves in the forest, determined to carry out our role as its custodians, to keep the area wild and free for ourselves and future generations.

As winter approached, we recognized the need to maintain a constant vigil in the Donaldson River Valley. We had been assured that road clearing and construction would be put on hold until spring, but a few months earlier, given similar assurances, we had left the valley only to find that the contractors had made a full-scale advance in our absence. In an effort to gain as much ground as possible, their bulldozers had made a beeline across the button grass plains from both the north and the south, trashing each stand of forest encountered. Up until then, they had been slowly moving forward, building the road as they went. Now they moved quickly, cutting a swathe without hindrance into the very heart of the Tarkine: the Donaldson River and its surrounding rain forest. We knew that the road had to be stopped before it reached the river; once the Donaldson could be driven over, all was pretty much lost. The bridge, we all recognized, was the last stand. Visions of the pristine riverbank being used by day-tripping tourists, who would leave behind their trash and, worse still, throw empty bottles into the river, strengthened our resolve that such places should be left out of reach of those who afforded them no respect. *Let them go and have a picnic somewhere else; somewhere where the damage has already been done.* We were determined to stop that from happening, and we weren't taking any chances. We would maintain a presence in the forest over winter, basing a crew in the bush for a week at a time on a rotating basis.

My shift had come around again. I left Weldborough, where I was house-sitting for Chris and Ebi while they were in Germany again, early one frosty morning, and drove across the state—for the umpteenth time—to the small midwestern town of Nabageena. Paul Clarke and Michelle Foale live in a house Paul built on a small piece of land surrounded by plantation forest and farmland, where he maintains the property as an oasis of natural bushland. Paul offered to drive me in to the drop-off point on the Tarkine's fringe. He was to pick up a group of four young guys, in the forest on their first visit to the area, so we could kill two birds with one stone. First, though, we had to detour to the west's largest town, Smithton (or 'Mifton, as it was affectionately known amongst our group), to pick up a guy named Jarrah, who would be coming into the forest for the first time. I always enjoyed taking people on their first visit to the Tarkine; seeing the wonder in their eyes, knowing they were experiencing something magical.

Finding Jarrah wasn't a problem. When you've got dreadlocks, a conservative town like Smithton is not an easy place to hide in. And with the three of us squashed into the front of Paul's small truck, we then filled Jarrah in on what had been happening so far. Actively involved in the North East Forest Action Group (NEFA) in New South Wales, Jarrah had seen plenty of forest action before, and he had heard on the grapevine what was happening in the Tarkine. He'd come down to see it first-hand, then to work out what he could do to help.

An hour and a half later, where the forestry road became no more than a dirt path, we reached the beginning of our secret access trail. The government had declared the entire area an off-limits construction zone, posting security guards at either end of the new road to deny access to the front line. We needed to get large numbers of people into the area without detection. There at the trailhead, cold and wet, were the four guys waiting to be picked up. They were still running on a high from their experience in this wild place. Eyes wide, they assured us we wouldn't believe how hard it was going to be to hike into base camp. I looked at Paul, smiling as I replied, "I reckon I might have a bit of an idea." I'd helped build base camp.

"How come there's only four of you? Aren't there supposed to be five?" asked Paul. One member of the previous week's party, a guy called Roger, had decided to stay in the bush for another shift. He would have been on his own for a few days before the next group—these guys—arrived, but he was to have left with them today. Maybe he'd wanted to stay for another shift . . .

"We heard there was going to be someone in camp already, but we never saw him. We found a sleeping bag and some other gear, but there was no sign of anybody," one of them said.

"Shit! Did you look for him at all?" asked Paul.

"Yeah, we walked around calling out for ages, but eventually figured that he must have left," someone else replied.

"Why would he leave behind all his gear like that?" I questioned, knowing the obvious answer, but trying to understand their reasoning.

Paul answered for me: "If he'd gotten himself lost or injured," he said gravely.

We all stood in silence as the reality of the situation began to sink in.

"We need to get in there straight away," I said to Paul, looking to Jarrah for his approval. This wasn't going to be the walk in the park that we'd planned. We were going to have to get in and out as fast as possible.

"I'll meet you back here at the same time tomorrow," Paul added. "If you're not here, I'm going to have to call the police to organize a search party."

"Try phoning around in Hobart [the state's capital] first," I replied. "He may have walked out and be sitting in a café there right now."

"OK. You guys'd better get moving. It's late. I'll be on the phone as soon as I get home to see what I can find out," he replied, clipping the tarp down on the tray of the truck. Jarrah and I adjusted our packs and climbed the log that hid the beginning of the trail. "Good luck!" Paul called out behind us, and we were on our way.

The trail we used had been cut a few months earlier and was difficult to follow in places. Our progress was slow. Despite the steady pace we kept, we were still in the forest as the sun began to set. Finally, we walked out onto a button grass plain in near darkness. We erected the tent quickly on a cushion of grass, had a quick meal of pasta, and climbed into the tent.

The next morning, as the first rays of light crept across the plain, we wolfed down breakfast, Jarrah's eyes open wide at his first view of the Tarkine: the button grass plains spread out below us, cut by fingers of forested valleys running down the slopes of the Norfolk Range in the distance. Standing out markedly was the ugly white scar of the road now under construction, which cut across the plains, breaking the pristine landscape.

Packing up camp, we set off, soon dropping into the first of many gullies that make traveling in this kind of terrain difficult. Filled with waist-high scrub and cutting grass, the gullies slowed our progress considerably, but we pushed on. On reaching the road, we found little relief, as we struggled along what the recent rain had turned into a continuous quagmire. "How are they going to maintain this?" I asked myself, pushing forward in knee-deep mud.

Hours later, we reached the opening cut into the tall band of forest that signalled our entry into the Donaldson Valley. Just inside the tree line, we left the road and made our way through the open forest to our first camp. Forrest Whitten and Ben Rae had built the hut a month earlier from salvaged bark, and it was a work of art. Jarrah was still admiring their handiwork and the extent of our establishment in the forest, when I heard, above the wind whistling through the trees, the sound of a helicopter approaching.

"C'mon, mate," I said to Jarrah, as I ran back to the road. "I don't want the police to know about this place at all." I figured that if we met them on the road they'd have no clue we'd just been in one of our camps. But no sooner had we started back toward the plain than four figures appeared on the rise, walking down toward us. I immediately recognized one as Paul, and felt that sinking feeling as the implications became obvious. The other three were police, and they didn't look happy. Sure enough, as they reached us, Paul, looking even more stressed than he had the night before, said to me, "He's not in Hobart, Wazza. Nobody's seen him."

"Shit!" was all I managed to say before one of the officers stepped forward and, without even introducing himself, said, "OK, you guys are going to help us search for this guy. You shouldn't be in here anyway, but since you are, you're going to show us every one of your little hiding places. Every camp. Everything! If I find out that you've held out on us, there'll be all hell to pay!"

"OK. *You've made that fairly clear,*" I thought to myself.

"Now, where are we going to start?" he barked.

"Apparently his sleeping bag is at our camp down by the river," I replied. (I presumed he was the chief; he certainly acted like he was.)

"Let's go then," the chief ordered, and we all started toward the Donaldson. As we walked, calling out the whole time, the chief kept reminding us of how much trouble we'd be in if we didn't cooperate fully.

Leading them straight to the Donaldson River campsite, I reflected on the measures we'd taken to keep its location secret. Covering our tracks whenever we came or went had paid off whenever the police tried to find the camp. Now we had to lead them directly to it.

Seeing Roger's bedding laid out under the tarp, his pack alongside, drove home the reality of what was happening. I thought of all the possibilities. It was winter. Temperatures below freezing are common at that time of year, and it rains a lot. No one would leave behind a sleeping bag out there—not on purpose. He could have slipped and injured himself in some way. He could easily have become lost.

We split up and searched the vicinity of the camp. I was looking for a body. If Roger had been out in this sort of weather for a week without warm clothes or a sleeping bag, he was dead, I'd decided. Peering under logs, brushing aside clumps of bracken, I expected a corpse to stare back at me at any moment.

One of the rescue guys used our tree ladder to gain some height so he could radio their chopper. Ironically, we had built the ladder to spot helicopters. They were used to drop contractors with chainsaws directly into the forest, so we had to know where they were. As soon as we knew one was landing, we would race to the area and make our presence known. The loggers were under orders to stop work if any protesters were seen, for safety reasons.

"I know of one more place to look," I suggested. "Down at the river they've been dropping some pretty big trees. It's dangerous in there, the fallen trees haven't settled yet, anything could happen."

"OK, you've got fifteen minutes," the chief said to Jarrah and I. "Take this with you." He handed Jarrah a hand-held two-way radio, briefly explained how to use it, then, as we turned to leave, added, "If you guys disappear on me, there'll be hell to pay!" Paul stayed with the police to help them search the original survey track, which we all (the Tigers) still used in preference to the road.

Climbing over and amongst the swathe of fallen trees, Jarrah and I peered into the tangled mess of branches, calling out constantly, expecting to see the worst. The helicopter circled overhead; as we approached the clearing, it sounded like it was landing. We were moving as quickly as possible, but progress was still agonizingly slow through the dense brush. We looked at each other in surprise as the drone of the helicopter's engine turned into a high pitched whine and it lifted off! Minutes later, we reached the clearing. It was empty.

"What do you think they're doing?" I asked Jarrah.

"I don't know," he replied. "Maybe they've gone back up onto the button grass."

After waiting five minutes, we began making our way back to the plain to meet them there, slightly pissed that they'd not waited for us at the riverbank or radioed us their change of plan. Jarrah called repeatedly down into the gully below: "Cooooooooooeeeee!" then stopped, listening for a reply. I really thought he was wasting his time. *He's dead. There's no way he'll still be alive if he's been lost all this time.*

Suddenly, Jarrah stopped in front of me. "Did you hear that?" he whispered, frowning.

"Did I hear what?"

"Listen," he said, then called again. "Cooooooooooeee!"

I strained my ears, trying to hear anything above the wind hissing through the trees. Nothing.

"Did you hear that?" he asked excitedly, looking into my eyes for confirmation.

"No. I didn't hear anything, except for the wind," I replied, sure he was imagining things.

"I'm sure I heard something. Listen again," he pleaded, then he called even louder this time: "Cooooooooooeeee!"

Standing with my head cocked to one side, left ear facing down into the gully, my heart skipped a beat as I heard the faint reply.

"Did you hear that?" Jarrah grabbed my arm.

"I did. I heard something." My heart was racing. We both called out this time and, sure enough, heard the faint reply again. "Cooooooooeeee!"

"He's alive!" I announced out loud, in total disbelief.

We took a compass bearing of the direction the voice came from: fifty-eight degrees from where we stood. At that moment, Paul appeared.

"We've found him!" Jarrah and I both yelled out at once, much to Paul's astonishment.

"Where are the cops?" I asked Paul. He explained that they'd flown back to Savage River, unable to wait for us any longer.

"That's the shortest fifteen minutes I've ever seen!" I replied in amazement. "They didn't even wait for us!"

"The radio," Jarrah exclaimed, holding it up. "We can get them on this!"

Jarrah held in the radio's "Talk" button and called "Ground crew to helicopter. Over." The radio replied with nothing but static.

"I've got to get to higher ground," announced Jarrah. "Then I should be able to get a signal."

"We've got to get down there," said Paul, looking to me. I nodded in agreement. "We need to get him some food and warm clothing."

"In the dark?" Jarrah queried, sounding concerned, the sun now below the horizon.

"I'm not going to be able to just lie down and sleep now that I know he's down there," I snapped.

"I know that, but you haven't stopped all day. At least have something to eat before you go," he reasoned. Jarrah had a point. I was running on adrenaline only, and that wouldn't last forever.

Looking down into the gully one last time, I tried to imagine what must be going through the guy's mind—how he must have felt as he realized we'd heard him. And now, what he was thinking, knowing we were leaving again? Would he know we were coming straight back? Would he resign himself to another night alone, comforted, albeit slightly, that he'd been found, that he might be saved?

Jarrah ran ahead, hoping to get a message to the chopper before it was too far away. Paul and I hiked back to the bark hut and began putting together the equipment we'd need. As Paul cooked some pasta and soup to take with us in a Thermos, I ran out to the road and up the hill to the button grass looking for Jarrah. I found him at the top of the next rise in a scene I'll never forget. In an effort to gain more height, he'd dragged a discarded 166-liter (44-gallon) drum into the center of the road and stood it on end. Balanced precariously on top of it, he was announcing loudly and slowly into the radio held against his mouth: "Hobart! Hobart! This is bark hut rescue. Do you read me? Over."

Amongst the static, a barely discernible voice could be made out in reply, but Jarrah was unsure whether they had received his message.

"It's no use, mate. They're not going to be able to do anything anyway, not until morning," I stated. "Paul and I are going down there."

"OK," he replied. "Good luck."

As I raced back into the forest I could still hear "Hobart! Hobart!"

Standing on the thin survey trail looking down into the darkness below, I felt like I was about to embark on a night dive. We were on the side of a ridge that dropped down at forty-five degrees through dense rain forest. The flashlight beam, which we used to search for a break in the undergrowth, failed to penetrate more than a few meters into the tangle of horizontal shrub.

I pulled down hard on my shoulder straps, drawing the pack tightly against my back, and looked across at Paul. He nodded his readiness. Setting the compass bearing at fifty-eight degrees, I then stepped forward. "OK, this is it. Let's do it."

We literally dropped off the trail into the dark before we were stopped almost immediately by the first barrier of scrub. Horizontal, as the name implies, grows horizontally, and vertically, and every angle in between. This creates an almost impenetrable web, tangled in on itself in the forest undergrowth. Climbing through any gaps we could fit through, we made our way forward, trying to retain our bearings. With the cord firmly drawn around my wrist, the flashlight swung free whenever I had to use both hands (which was often), the beam dancing wildly across the ferns and moss beneath my feet. I'd become accustomed to moving through this type of terrain over the last few months. At first, I'd been completely freaked out by the claustrophobic feeling of barely being able to move, as my clothes and pack constantly got hooked up in the stuff. It didn't faze me this time. We were on a mission.

Stopping to check the compass and pick out our next landmark, I called out "Coooooooooeeeee!"

The response was immediate; clearer now that the wind had died down. Urged on, we picked up the pace, sometimes falling as rotting logs gave way under our feet. In sections the forest opened up, allowing us to move faster. Roger's response became louder and louder as we moved closer. Calling continuously, we were talking to him now, telling him it was OK, that we had him.

We had traveled less than a kilometer from the trail when we finally reached him. Calling out the last time, his response had come from straight ahead, but as I scanned around in front of me, I could see nothing. It wasn't till I leant down to look under a huge rotted-out log that I saw him—staring back at me from the darkness with wild eyes. He reminded me of a scared, wounded animal.

"Mate. Am I glad to see you!" I said, as I worked my pack off. I reached under the log and took his arm. It was soaking wet, and cold.

No sooner had we introduced ourselves than he staggered me by asking, "Have you guys got any tobacco? I could do with a smoke."

"No, we haven't, mate. But I've got some hot soup here if you'd like some."

As he sipped the broth, we asked him what had happened, how he had ended up down here. He recounted how he had left one of the campsites (we had several) to get some coffee from another. It was imperative that we stay hidden in the forest, so we were all very careful to avoid leaving tracks that could alert the police to our whereabouts. Roger had simply become disoriented between the two camps, and soon found himself lost. For days he had wandered, attempting to find his way back. With only a handful of oats in one pocket, he'd been too scared to eat. After finding this log, he'd sheltered under it for a couple of days before hearing the helicopter yesterday afternoon. He had gone down to the river (which was down an embankment, just below us) and waded into the middle to try and attract attention. It was now a full eight days since he'd set out to get the coffee, and he still had the oats in his pocket.

At first, I was amazed at how casual Roger was about the whole situation, and left Paul to tend to him while I looked for a place to pitch the tent. I realized later that he must have had to psyche himself up incredibly to deal with his seemingly hopeless situation. He had convinced himself that he was OK, rather than face the soul-destroying possibility of dying cold and alone under a sodden log.

Using a tomahawk, I hacked a space within the web of horizontal on what looked like the only available piece of level ground. I managed to erect the tent in there, by which time Paul had set Roger—still under the log—up with another cup of hot soup. His feet looked terrible, swollen and cut from walking barefoot. He hadn't worn shoes when he set off for coffee, preferring to go without, but that choice had turned against him. The Tasmanian bush is extreme, and the constant damp in the rain forest had softened his feet. He had wrapped them in what looked like the sleeves of his shirt, but they were cut so badly that the blood had seeped through.

Roger finally agreed to come out from under the log; it had provided him with relative shelter and comfort these past few days, and he was obviously apprehensive about leaving. We both carried him to the tent, Paul crawling inside with him to arrange his sleeping bag. I spread my bag out under "Roger's log," then wormed my way into the bag for what was, up to that point, the most uncomfortable sleep of my life. I couldn't believe Roger had lasted so long under there. I was wet within half an hour from the water leaking out of the moss all around me. Luckily I had a Dacron (synthetic) sleeping bag or I would have frozen. I tossed and turned all night, feeling completely claustrophobic, the dank underside of the log only centimeters from my face. But I felt humbled by the experience, *determined* to sleep under there. *He's been under here for that long with only the clothes on his back. Surely I can handle one night.*

Inside the tent, Paul spent all night huddled up to Roger, hugging him to keep him warm. Paul told me later how he feared he might lose him, with Roger slipping into a fever as he warmed up, his body shivering uncontrollably.

I woke from my semi-sleep at first light to the sound of a chopper. Racing down to the river, I stepped out onto the rocks and waved my arms to flag it down. The pilot spotted me immediately and, after circling a few more times, proceeded to lower the first of three crew down onto an exposed rock near the river's edge. It was an incredible sight, the giant steel hummingbird hovering perfectly still between the trees on either side of the river. As soon as the fellow on the line touched down, he unclipped from the rope, freeing it up for the next guy. He then made his way over the rocks to where I stood on the bank. He introduced himself as a paramedic and enquired after Roger's whereabouts and condition.

"Follow me, he's just up here." I led him up the steep bank through the thick scrub to our makeshift camp.

As the paramedic tended to Roger, the chief appeared, and he wasn't happy. "What happened to you guys yesterday? Didn't I tell you not to disappear?" he barked.

Angry at his accusation, I replied, "You didn't wait for us. That wasn't fifteen minutes!"

"And what did you think you were doing coming down here in the dark like that? Look at the danger you've put yourselves in! We could have ended up searching for you as well this morning!" he ranted.

"We've been in here for months, mate! Do you think we would have come down here if we didn't think we could do it? Look at the gear we've brought down with us," I said, motioning toward the Tomahawk, the Thermos of soup. If he was furious with us, I was furious too—with his attitude.

When he finished ranting shortly afterward and stepped away, the paramedic turned to me and said, "Don't take too much notice of him. You guys did the right thing and you did it well. Don't worry about what he says, he's just pissed off at the whole episode. As far as I'm concerned, you guys have done the rescue, we're just taking him out."

Paul and I stood back, feeling much better at the recognition of our efforts, as the paramedic went about stabilizing Roger, getting him ready for the stretcher. He was in a lot worse condition than had first been apparent, suffering badly from exposure and hypothermia. I didn't think he would have lasted much longer if he hadn't been found. After he'd been strapped into the fiberglass stretcher, we all helped carry him down the steep bank to the river and across the rocks to the point where the helicopter hovered overhead.

As Roger was winched up into the waiting bird, then whisked away, I made my way back up the steep slope, through the bracken and dogwood, to our makeshift camp. Quickly packing up the tent, I stuffed everything into my pack, ready for a quick escape. Our work was finished.

"I'll see you guys later on. You don't need me any more," I announced. I knew Paul would have to go back in the chopper, not having his pack, but I wanted to get back to the camp.

"Where do you think you're going?" the angry one barked.

"I've got to go back and pick up some gear, do a few things," I replied.

"Not that way you're not," he snapped.

"Why not?" I asked, truly angry, "How do you think I got here?"

"I don't care, mate. I can't let you go back that way. What if something happens to you? How good is that going to look for us?" he said, obviously enjoying himself.

"Hey, I came down there in the dark. I reckon I might be able to get back in broad daylight!" I replied sarcastically.

"Forget it! You're coming with us!"

We found Roger after they shot through, and now we're being treated like amateurs!

I was far from happy. Everyone moved down toward the riverbank, and I saw my chance to bolt. But the chief stood waiting for me. "C'mon, mate, we're leaving."

"Yeah, I'll be down there in a sec. I'm just going to have a piss," I replied, moving over to an appropriate spot.

This was my chance. I had my pack on. *As soon as I've had this piss, I'm out of here.*

I turned to find him standing right beside me, waiting.

"You right there, mate?" I enquired.

"Finish your piss and let's go."

I still wanted to make a run for it, just take off into the bush. But my pack was heavy with all the extra gear we'd brought along for Roger.

He may be a slow, fat bastard, but I'm not going to be able to move through this horizontal too quickly with a heavy pack on.

"Yeah, all right," I replied, agitated that he had me. He followed me down to the riverbank all the way, and I began to regret having not run for it immediately.

The chopper eventually returned from delivering Roger to a waiting ambulance and winched us up one at a time. The forest looked incredible from up in the air, seeming to go on forever. I was mesmerized by the colors. I'd never seen so many variations of green, individual trees standing out distinctly in the crowd.

Then, on the horizon, *Jesus Christ!* A huge clearing ahead looked like a piece of forest had been ripped up like a piece of turf. Before us yawned the gaping hole of the Savage River Mine. As we got closer I peered down into the toxic green tailing dams below, the ones that occasionally spill over and run straight into the Savage River. Huge machinary tore away at the earth as I watched, and the enormity of our struggle hit home.

We truly are living in a world gone mad. Why have we got no respect for the earth? Why have we got no connection?

When did we lose it? The question filled my head as we descended toward a large gas station car park in the township of Savage River. There, Paul and I received the full-on interrogation at the local police station before being driven in to Burnie, two hours away, for more of the same. As I stepped out of the police jeep in the heart of town, the officer looked me up and down, smiling, "So, do you always come into town in your underwear?" (I hadn't bothered with expensive thermal gear at that stage of my hiking career; I just made do with a pair of long johns I'd picked up for a few dollars.)

"Yeah, no worries. I'm not really supposed to be in town, remember!" I replied, sick of the whole situation. We hadn't done anything wrong and we were being treated like criminals. I felt a deep sadness that this is what we had come to, our so called "civilized" society. The very fact that we even had to be out there to protect such an area appalled me. As I had explained to a hostile woman in a Burnie pub one afternoon, I had better things to do with my life. I'd rather have been getting on with living than be going through confrontation after confrontation, which gets depressing after a while. But I, like all the others, simply couldn't stand idly by after seeing what was happening in there. We had been deeply moved by nature and treated like criminals for heeding its call.

Still, thinking about the whole episode later, I realized what I'd gained from the experience with Roger. It reinforced for me that I was competent in the wild. Jumping off that trail with Paul was like crossing into another realm; he felt it too. We had gone to the outer limits of our comfort zones in order to bring back someone who had gone too far. And I'd seen first-hand the resilience of the human spirit: the way Roger had raised himself up mentally to survive. He had had to believe he was OK, otherwise he would have just slipped into the void and slowly gone mad or become hysterical at the enormity of his situation. Talking himself up was the only way he could have held himself together. I had experienced only a fraction of his ordeal by sleeping under his log.

They were important lessons to learn, more important than I could have imagined at the time. For lying under "my" rock years later, it would be those experiences with Roger that I would draw upon: knowing I was strong enough, that I'd been tested before, that I had to hold it together to avoid slipping into that same black void that Roger had been staring into when we found him under that log.

Found

Am I still dreaming? Am I still alive? Can I hear a helicopter?

It sounds like it's getting louder.

Yes!

Instantly awake now, I feel my pulse quicken. I grab the poly tarp and quickly unfold it, my eyes frantically scanning the sky for a sign. The noise *is* getting louder.

Please God, let it be looking for me.

Suddenly, out of the blue sky, like a dragonfly in the distance, a helicopter.

Yes, they're looking for me! Yes!

My heart almost jumps out of my chest.

Over here! I'm over here!

Holding the tarp up high, waving it steadily back and forth so as to keep it floating at its maximum size, I pray for the chopper to come closer. Even though I can see it, I know from past experience with helicopters that the pilot will find it difficult to see me down in this gully. It needs to be directly over me, and it's far from that at the moment, apparently following another gully to the southeast. Finally, it's heading this way, until eventually it's almost directly over me at a height of about 50 meters (160 feet).

"Here! I'm down here!" But it keeps going, checking another gully to the northeast, over toward "The Thumb."

Then it's off, heading toward the coast. Filled with a mixture of elation and despair, I still don't know whether it's seen me or not.

It should have circled me, shouldn't it?

I struggle with the concept of the pilot not seeing me before realizing: *They're looking for me. Of that I'm certain!*

The next five or ten minutes are the longest of my life, before the giant chopper appears again, this time heading straight toward me. It stops directly above, swirling leaves and debris around me before tilting forward and swooping in a wide circle. I can see someone at the window inside.

Are they giving me the thumbs up? The chopper circles again before turning toward the coast.

Where the bloody hell are they going?

It doesn't matter, they've seen me. I slump back on my Therm-a-rest as if a huge weight has been lifted from my shoulders. No matter what happens now, I'm no longer alone.

The Rescue

The sight of the returning helicopter is one that will stick with me forever . . . flying directly toward me, circling once before taking up a position 100 meters (330 feet) downstream; hovering perfectly, like a giant dragonfly, over one of the few clearings on the river. The wind generated is incredible. I can only sneak quick glances as leaves, dust, and water are blown all around me, the wind roaring along with the beating and chopping of the rotor blades. I'm well aware of how dangerous this is and close my mind to thoughts of anything else going wrong.

Catching glimpses of another human being lowered into the middle of the creek bed, I feel so grateful for technology. He looks immensely professional, walking carefully toward me, checking me out as would a hunter approaching a wounded animal—assessing the situation, with both me and my surroundings.

"My name is Chip Jaffurs. I'm a doctor," he shouts. His American accent is unmistakable, even above the roar of the rotors. "How are you doing?"

"I'm all right, mate. Am I glad to see you!"

Chip crouches beside me, setting his case on some rocks alongside. (Later I'll learn that he is an emergency medicine specialist with more than 10 years' experience.) Opening his case as we speak, he asks the first of many questions.

"Are you in pain?"

"No," I reply. "Not any more."

"How long have you been here?"

"Since Wednesday."

"When did you last eat?"

"Yesterday, I think. I've been throwing up all day."

"When did you last drink?"

"This morning?" I answer, but it's more of a question to myself.

"Are you allergic to any drugs?"

"No, none that I know of."

Finding that my systolic blood pressure (the pressure in my arteries as the heart pumps blood through them) is extremely low (a result of dehydration and shock), he puts together a 60-mmHg intravenous line with a cannula the size of a knitting needle. He confidently finds a vein, then pushes, rather than slides, the needle in. Through the line, he then introduces morphine, followed by antinausea medication. He then washes the ants off my legs with cups of water. I've long forgotten about them, but apparently they've been having quite a picnic. A wave of warmth and well-being sweeps over me as the morphine takes hold.

The chopper is hovering just downstream, lowering crewman Dany Portefaix and airport fire officer Bill Johnstone into the creek. They have with them a hydraulic jack, a crowbar, and a couple of stepped wooden blocks. With all the gear off-loaded, the helicopter then leaves the scene, returning to the beach to conserve fuel. Chip changes the bag of fluid feeding the IV in my left arm from antinausea medication to the first of what will be a total of 6 liters (1.5 gallons) of saline and Hartmans solution (electrolyte/dextrose). Its purpose is to raise my blood pressure and minimize the risk of kidney failure when the weight of the rock is released. Under his instructions, I hold the bag up with my right hand, careful to keep it higher than the point at which the cannula has pierced my vein, so gravity can assist the flow. Within minutes I can barely hold the bag up, I feel so weak, so tired. I feel myself slipping away. With a start, I realize I've dozed off and that the bag is in my lap.

"Keep the bag up high, Warren. Otherwise it could start to run backward and you'll be losing fluid. Try squeezing it under your arm; just be sure to keep pressure on it." I find this much easier, though within minutes I'm dozing off again, relaxed no doubt from the combination of morphine and relief at no longer being alone.

I'm in a bit of a haze as I'm greeted by Dany and Bill. They quickly introduce themselves, then quiz me on exactly what happened while they assess the rock and how it's positioned on me. I explain how, because it's broken into two pieces, the weight is spread over the full length of my legs, requiring the rock to be lifted straight up rather than from one end. They have obviously decided on a plan, and begin laying out equipment nearby.

Once Chip is satisfied he has me stabilized, he pulls out a video camera. "Do you mind if we film this, Warren?"

I've got no problem with being filmed, as long as they can get me out. "No worries, mate. Are you going to use it on one of those TV rescue shows?"

"No, not quite. We use rescue videos in training to demonstrate the use of a particular piece of equipment and to help us back up funding requests. At times, the government gets a bit tight-fisted with the funding for equipment, and we find it helpful to have evidence of where its money has been spent—how it has been used for specific rescues."

I'm praying these guys know what they're doing with this gear because, in a way, I'm not looking forward to the rock being lifted at all. *What if it falls again?* The mere thought makes me shudder. I know that if the rock falls on me again, I will want to die.

It's not that easy, though, is it? What will I do, just hold my breath?

Chip checks my blood pressure again. It's steady at a much healthier 110 mmHg systolic now.

"Are you guys ready?" he asks Dany and Bill.

"Yes, we're ready."

This is a critical point in the operation. All the toxins, plus the potassium that has built up in my legs from the lack of circulation, will be released back into my bloodstream as soon as the pressure is released. Chip gives me a shot of adrenaline to get my heart racing and hopefully move any clots through quickly.

They start with the jack positioned under the right-hand side of the rock, where Bill slowly pumps the handle up and down while Dany lifts with the crowbar to my left. Very slowly, almost imperceptibly, the pressure begins to ease on my right leg as Bill pumps. I feel an increase in the pressure on my left as most of the weight is transferred to that leg. I try to ignore it, but can't.

"Jesus, that hurts," is all I can manage in response to the pain.

Dany counters the pressure with the crowbar, while Bill quickly places a wooden chock beside the jack before lowering it slowly so that the bulk of the weight settles onto the chock. Bill moves the jack over to my left, changes over the contact plate, then sets it into position before beginning again. From side to side they work, with me drifting in and out of consciousness along the way a number of times. (Later, Chip tells me that he was sure he was going to lose me at this point, but I somehow managed to come back.) All I feel is a huge sense of relief at being able to sleep while they work. If there's a light at the end of a tunnel, I don't see it. If this is dying, it doesn't seem any different from falling asleep. It is actually quite peaceful.

With the rock poised about 10 centimeters (4 inches) above me now, the first attempt is made to get me out. We quickly encounter the problem that would have made it so difficult, even if Geert and I had been able to lift the rock, to actually get me out from underneath. I'm lying back against a step in the rock. This means I need to have enough clearance between the rock and my legs to allow my bum to be lifted up and over the step. So the guys continue lifting until the rock is about 20 centimeters (8 inches) above my legs, looming precariously over me. I'm desperately trying not to think about the consequences of it falling now. *No, it can't happen.*

"OK, are we ready to go?" Dany calls, crouching behind me, his arms around my waist, fingers locked together. As he lifts, Bill monitors the jack and chocks while Chip looks after the lines trailing from me. I'm pushing with all my might to help Dany as much as I can, which astounds Chip. He's just watched me return from the dead.

Freedom

"Get the hell off me!" I groan, as Dany drags me back till my legs are clear.

An enormous sense of freedom engulfs me. I can't move my legs at all, but the satisfaction of pushing out from under there is huge. Even if I haven't actually done much, I think it is more the symbolic act in itself, finally pushing the weight off me after all this time, that brings an immediate sense of relief.

I'm loaded straight onto a stretcher and covered with a space blanket before being strapped in tight in preparation for being winched into the chopper. The helicopter has just returned, and Chip signals it before realizing it's not ours. It's the paparazzi, complete with a bright spotlight and the obligatory cameraman hanging out the side. Chip angrily waves them off and, within minutes, they're replaced by the real thing.

It's all too clear how dangerous this is. If the stretcher starts to spin during winching, cutting the winch line is sometimes the only option available to protect the chopper. Riding up with me is Chip, flashlight clenched between his teeth, beam flashing erratically across the scene below. Dany's holding the stabilizing line below us. It's almost completely dark now, a few minutes later and they would have had to abort the rescue, leaving Chip with me for the night. He's glad that hasn't happened because, as he tells me later, there's no doubt in his mind I wouldn't have lasted the night.

Inside, the chopper is almost as noisy as it was from the outside. I don't notice for long, though. I slip into unconsciousness even before Dany and Bill are winched up with all their tools. Chip has got me rigged up to a monitor as the pilot, Tim Kesteven, lifts us out of the gully, turning toward Cairns Base Hospital. We cross the island in a couple of minutes, over the Hinchinbrook Channel, then on to Tully for refuelling. We arrive at the hospital at 8:39 PM on Friday, April 11, 1997.

GEERT VAN KEULEN: *Friday morning, April 11, 1997*
After a horrible night (I can't remember much of it but do know it was a bad trip), I packed my gear for the last time. A few droplets of a small shower fell on the tent. It was overcast and cold. I managed to put some muesli in my mouth, but was stiff and sore all over my body. At 5:30 AM I washed myself in the ocean, dressed, and had a snack. Slowly I packed my rucksack with stiff and sore fingers, swung it over my shoulders and started my struggle toward the jetty, the starting point of the trek. I knew that I should be able to make it to the jetty in three or four hours, where I hoped to catch the first tourist boat of the day. It was sheer agony, but I finally got there just before 10 AM.

There were two hikers at the boat launch, from Queensland, who had walked the trail from the opposite direction and were waiting for the boat to take them back to Cardwell. When I saw them on the far end of a sandy clearing in the mangroves, I waved, then realized that most of my voice had disappeared. I was afraid they wouldn't believe my desperate need for help. After all, my story was going to sound pretty unbelievable.

In staccato and with a lot of difficulty, I explained to them what had happened. My tongue seemed to have lost its function. It was glued to my palate. Words came out very slowly. I was extremely thirsty and asked for water; one of the guys gave me his water bottle. Water never tasted better. Then one of them went to the beach with me and we collected firewood, paper, and plastic that had been washed ashore so we could build a fire, creating thick, black smoke. With a long stick he drew a message in the smooth layer of sand: "SOS. MAN TRAPPED UNDER ROCK FOR 36 HOURS" in letters about 1 meter (3.5 feet) in size, to attract a plane.

One of the guys stayed at the jetty to warn us as soon as a boat came in. They expected one at noon, but at noon there was still no boat. Once again, my patience was tested. I passed the time sitting or lying on the beach, trying to sleep or spot Warren's position on Mount Bowen. For me, all the beauty of the mountain had disappeared.

The two Aussies then also ran out of water, and I strolled back down the long beach of Ramsay Bay to find a freshwater stream where I could drink and fill the water bottles. It was a fair walk, and I was annoyed that neither of the two offered to get some water for me. One of them continued to just hang around on the jetty, though the other one was much more active and aware of the precariousness of the situation. But I didn't feel like arguing, and went. The walk to the stream was hard, even without the pack, and just before reaching it I trod on a cane toad. It scared me; for an instant I thought I would break down. I filled my bottle, emptied it in my mouth, refilled it and the others, then wandered back to my waiting post, still not knowing when or if a boat would come in. It was very possible that it wouldn't because the bad weather might keep the boats wisely ashore. Maybe no more tourists would arrive today? But the two Queenslanders had booked their trip in advance, so one should come.

Half an hour before I left Warren, he had told me that he could hold out one more night but not a second. If a rescue party could not get him out before nightfall the next day, he said, he was sure he was going to die. The calm composure with which he told me this made such an impact on me that I could not doubt his feelings. I was sure he had an immaculate sense of timing and complete understanding of his own strengths. (Later, at the hospital, he told me that he knew if we got him out from underneath the rock after the long hours of work, he would have had a big chance of dying. Acid builds up in the blood after the circulation is cut off for a long time, and it could have poisoned him. He would certainly have had thrombosis. But he had to get out as the water rose, and his pain and sense of complete helplessness were much stronger than the impulse to do nothing and wait.) Walking back to the area near the fire and the message, I thought about his words.

AS I APPROACHED the area where I had been resting, I saw one of the hikers waving to me. I managed to walk a bit faster, to hurry toward a very serious and helpful boatman. The two Aussies had already explained the situation, and the man was busy off-loading his tourists. He then took me on his boat. The man's name tag said "Goody," his nickname, I guess, and good he was. He sped with me back into the mangrove channels and out to the open sea. He was very professional and didn't doubt my words for a moment, but just went straight into action.

The open sea was the only place where Goody could put out a mayday, but, alas, his radio would still not transmit. The very beautiful Hinchinbrook Island and its Mount Bowen were in the way. But there were a few crab boats sheltering somewhere in the mangrove channels, and Goody started to look for them. Finally, after sailing through the channels for maybe half an hour, we found one. An old Hemingwayish character, a "crabby," came alongside when he spotted us and helped pull us on board. He looked like he'd walked off the set of an old movie: short, elephant skin, unshaven, gray-haired, and tough as a nail. We shook hands with him and he got out his cellphone. After trying several times for about fifteen minutes, he managed to contact the Hinchinbrook Resort, a Barrier Reef resort on another island nearby. I had written a list with information about where Warren was, what time the accident happened, the state of his spirits and his injuries; Goody slowly repeated the words to the operator on the resort. When this was done, we sailed back to the jetty, leaving Hemingway behind.

I thanked Goody for his help—an important link in the chain of Warren's rescue. He then took the two Aussies and two day-trippers back on board and left me behind on the beach. It was 2:30 PM and there I sat once more—waiting, impatient, on the same spot in the sand. New, threatening dark clouds gathered above Bowen. I rolled a cigarette and lay down, resting my head on my pack. It was very damaged: the straps were broken, the plastic joints, too, and the bottom part was ripped. My boots were also torn, on both sides. The pack had been on my back at high altitude in Nepal and had accompanied me on another hairy adventure in the Pyrenees Mountains in Spain. I felt very attached to it and vowed never to throw it away, the pack or the boots. I was sure my girlfriend would understand this time.

Three thirty. No helicopter yet. Where the hell were they? Time was really running out now. The SOS message was passed on nearly two hours ago. I was uncertain of myself and impatient. "Is Warren still alive? Is the chopper coming? Can I join them? Do I have to camp another night out here?" I told myself to calm down, that the waiting would soon end. Sometimes I dozed off, but the adrenaline was still pumping too hard for me to sleep properly. I kept scanning the air: east, west, and south from me—I expected a green army chopper, as both Townsville and Cairns have bases. Finally, at 4:30 PM, I saw a black fly hovering against the dark background of Mount Bowen. It circled there for maybe ten minutes, then came my way. I got up with incredible joy, took my sarong out of my pack, and started waving and trying to yell.

Up there in the chopper they must have spotted me straight away, with their trained eyes, but I wasn't sure. Then, when it was a few hundred meters (660 feet) away, the helicopter circled and flew toward me over the sand dunes. The wind nearly swept me into the Barrier Reef. It landed on the beach and two people got out, one crew, the other a policeman from Cardwell, dressed in blue overalls. He had guided the QES helicopter toward me. They both ran at me and, in my excitement, I threw my pack over my shoulders and attempted to run toward them. But the crewman waved a determined "No" to send me back.

The policeman walked away from me and sat down in the grass on the edge of the beach. The crewman, whose name was Greg Beer, put both his arms firmly around me and told me to bend my head. We then ran to the chopper. Or rather, he dragged me to the chopper while the wind from the rotors blew the fine sand in our faces. He guided me carefully, but very firmly, into the co-pilot's seat, then put a headset on my wildly tangled curls. Just before getting on board himself, he explained how I could communicate with the other members aboard.

I looked over my shoulder and saw four serious looking men studying me from the back of the helicopter. All were dressed in black overalls and wearing helmets with big black visors, and were strapped into harnesses. Sweat ran in straight lines down their faces. They looked focused, ready to do whatever it took to get Warren out. I turned to the pilot, who nodded in a friendly way to me. A little button on the floor near my right foot had to be pushed so I could hear the others and communicate with the crew. As soon as I worked it out, the doctor asked me about Warren's situation.

"How was he when you left him? How were his spirits?"

"Good when I left him," I answered.

The pilot flicked switches and turned dials, preparing for take-off. Sand blew around the helicopter and the noise of the engine came to a high pitch, then we were in the air. Crewman Dany, a strong, bearded Frenchman who'd grown up in Australia, showed me a crowbar and asked if they would be able to get him out with it. I shook my head. "No." The pilot asked me how to get to the accident site.

"Fly to the lagoon, follow the creek upward, and he should be a few hundred meters (660 feet) from a large cliff face," I told him. We flew very quickly over the headlands I'd crossed earlier, and in about ten to fifteen minutes we were almost there, circling with the chopper's right side toward the mountain. All of us looked with deep concentration into the green jungle below, then suddenly I heard Dany call, "I see him, he's waving his arm!"

"He's alive!"

Dany said more things, but I have forgotten them—forgotten them because I became quite emotional. Tears came, and I smiled and laughed. Finally, my emotions could be released.

After that, the chopper hovered around the site a bit. The crew took coordinates and established Warren's exact location, then the chopper turned and made its way back to Ramsay Bay. I decided to enjoy the ride back to the beach.

The cop was called Ian, and he was still waiting in the grass bordering the sand dunes when the rescue helicopter dropped me off. Looking at the sea, I felt tired, and, lost within my own thoughts, I stared off into the distance. After about ten minutes, another helicopter, which I never heard coming, appeared in front of us. It landed and out came a cameraman, a reporter, and the pilot of what, apparently, was a chartered helicopter—chartered by Channel Nine news.

"You're joking!" I thought, and before I knew it the reporter asked permission to interview me. I had no problems with that; in my mind Warren was alive and safe and I was overjoyed. I then walked 90 meters (300 feet) or so over the beach while they filmed me with the island—and Bowen in particular—in the background, but I would regret the interview later. It felt weird to say the least. The film crew then waited for the rescue helicopter to return, meanwhile filming as much as possible.

Finally, the rescue chopper was parked a few hundred meters (660 feet) away from me. It wasn't black or green, but bright red, white, and blue. Its rotor blades were bent down, slightly moving in the sea breeze. The crew seemed to be working out a plan before they flew back to the accident site. I wondered what Warren was thinking. First he would have seen the chopper hovering in search for him, then it left, to return with me on board some fifteen minutes later. And then it left once more to refuel on the mainland. Finally, it was going to return once again to drop off a few people. "Would he be thinking that they couldn't find him?" I wondered. It must have been a fantastic moment for him when he heard, then saw, the helicopter come around the mountain for the first time.

After half an hour, the rescuers went back to the accident site to start their long fight against the clock, the weather, and the darkness. My work was done.

The TV people filmed some of the operation from the air, then returned to Ian and me. They offered us a lift back to Cardwell, and we flew over the beach and filmed the message that had been drawn in the sand earlier in the day. Flying over Hinchinbrook Island, with the sun slowly setting, gave us quite majestic views. Knowing that Warren was being taken care of allowed me to enjoy the beauty of the place once more. From my seat in the back, I could see Mount Bowen, then we flew over the mangrove forests and the breathtaking Hinchinbrook Channel back to the coast. The crew chatted and discussed where they were going to spend the night, and it struck me that this was routine for them. I thought about Warren and my friend in Townsville, Rohan, and his wife, Trish. I longed for a friend. I felt the need to talk about the whole experience with someone I could trust. I was sure Rohan and Trish would fulfill that need.

The chopper landed on the football ground, from where a police car took me to Cardwell police station. I asked if I could take a shower at Ian's house, which he had told me was next door. Free of the sweat and filth of my body, I then waited back at the station to be taken to Townsville. I expected that a police report would need filling in. But that never happened. I chatted with Ian, who had dropped his macho façade, and to his assistant, as I relaxed a little. A local reporter connected to the *Townsville Bulletin* interviewed me and took a few photographs as I stood in front of a map of Hinchinbrook Island.

Minutes later, my senses were on full alert once more when a fellow walked in and announced that he was from the Marine Authority. He started asking questions in an authoritative, unfriendly way, and I realized that I needed to be cautious. My suspicions seemed well-founded when he asked repeatedly for my permit. "Who gave you the permit?" he kept asking. I told him I couldn't remember. I thought I had lost it, perhaps up on the mountain, or maybe it was still somewhere in my pack. But I certainly didn't feel like checking my pack for his sake.

Meanwhile I had developed a serious headache, and when he kept on nagging, I snarled: "Look, mate, I've just tried to save someone's life, am I in trouble or something?"

He backed off, and the copper quickly stepped in and said that if he was ever going to go hiking, he would ask me to join his party. Meanwhile, the reporter had made a deal with the newspaper in Townsville. The policemen would now take me in their car to Ingham, halfway between Cardwell and Townsville, together with the film that had been taken. From there, I would travel back to Townsville with another reporter from the newspaper. I picked up my backpack, threw it in the back of the cop car, and sat behind the plastic screen in the back seat, wondering what kind of people had sat in the same seat and in what condition. Ian and his mate chatted as I stared into the dark tropical night. At about 8 PM, the radio crackled, and someone in the chopper explained that Warren was in "stable condition" and on his way to the hospital in Cairns. I was thrilled.

At the police station in Ingham, the film and I were transferred to another car, which took me to Rohan's place.

"Make sure to drop by after a few days' rest," the reporter said. "We'd like to write about your reunion with Warren. We can organize transportation for you up to Cairns."

"Maybe," I said, and was soon knocking on Rohan's door.

I had frightened Rohan and Trish when I called them from the Cardwell police station, but they soon realized what I'd been through and they took care of me. We drank a little wine and scotch, chatted (I can't recall about what), and listened to some relaxing jazz until quite late.

A Stark Reality

I wake to the feeling of being lifted, and open my eyes to see that I'm surrounded by people in white. I didn't even know we'd landed. I feel like I'm on the roof of the hospital for some reason. (When I see the helipad for the first time three weeks later, it doesn't look familiar at all.) I'm transferred to a trolley, then wheeled in to the hospital. It all seems so dramatic. It doesn't occur to me that my condition is so serious. I'm floating on a sea of morphine and still overcome with relief at having actually been rescued. I can feel that I'm moving but can't make out anything outside of my own space, it's almost like I'm floating through a mist.

My vision comes back into focus and, this time, it looks like I'm in some kind of operating theater. More faces are looking down at me. *Are they the same people?* I can't tell. I'm so tired, I just want to sleep. It's almost like I'm feeling the pain not so much as actual pain, but as a heaviness caused by my energy having been drained from me. Someone is asking me questions, others are monitoring the equipment I am wired up to.

"What's your name?"

"Where do you live?" and so on. . . .

A woman introduces herself as Katherine Swanson, an orthopedic registrar. "We're going to have to let someone know what's happened to you, Warren. Is there anyone you'd like us to call?" she asks.

"Yeah, Dad would be best. I don't want to freak Mom out," I reply through the oxygen mask.

"OK, what's his name and phone number?"

I give her Dad's details.

"Now, would you like me to call him for you?"

"No. It's OK. I can do it," I reply.

"Are you sure? It might be better if I do it for you."

"OK." I'm nodding, eyes closed, realizing how hard it would be, unsure of how I'd get the words out if I heard Dad's voice—a voice I hadn't expected to ever hear again only a few hours ago. (Thinking about it later, I'm amazed she even gave me the option of calling myself.)

She disappears from my side, only to be replaced by a man this time. "Now, I'm going to touch you Warren. I want you to tell me when you feel anything, and where it is that you're feeling it."

"OK."

I'm looking up at the ceiling when he asks me the first time, "Can you feel this, Warren?"

I hesitate, not feeling anything. "No," I reply softly.

"What about this?" as he runs his finger higher up my leg.

"No. No. No. Maybe?" as he continues. *Did I feel something then or was it just my imagination?*

I look down as his fingers reach my penis. I hadn't noticed until now: it's swollen and twisted around like a corkscrew. I cringe at the sight of it, and a lump forms in my throat as he asks me, "What about this, can you feel anything now?"

"Yeah, sort of," I answer hesitantly, knowing full well that I didn't feel a thing. But I'm not giving anybody the green light to do anything hasty. (In retrospect, my response may well have made things a lot more complicated for me, but that was a chance I had to take. The possibility of losing my legs was one thing—but losing my penis as well. . . . I couldn't bear the thought.)

He obviously isn't taking my word for it anyway. He's holding up a length of plastic tubing with a bulbous end. "Now, Warren, this is going to be pretty uncomfortable, mate, but we need to make sure your urethra hasn't been damaged. I'm going to have to insert this into your penis." It looks like it's going to be more than uncomfortable. "OK," I reply, swallowing hard.

Wincing as he inserts the plastic intruder, I don't realize that the very fact that it feels so uncomfortable is a good sign. I do have feeling there—just.

"OK, Warren, that's fine."

Thank God for that.

I'm glad I can't see my legs clearly at this stage. The right knee is smashed and swollen; same with my left ankle. They've also turned blue and the skin has begun to slough off in sheets.

Another guy moves to my side, introducing himself in a voice so soft that I'm straining to hear him. "My name is Bill Clark, Warren. I'm a surgeon."

With absolute compassion, he explains the situation to me quietly.

"Your legs have been very badly damaged, Warren. The circulation has been cut off for almost forty-eight hours. The tissue has died. I'm afraid we can't save them."

Squeezing my eyes tightly shut, I try to comprehend what he's saying, what I've been shutting out since seeing the green spots on my right foot.

It's true, this is really happening.

"I'm sorry, Warren, but we're going to have to amputate both your legs."

My stomach knots, pulling my diaphragm up hard, forcing out a sniffling gasp as hot tears squeeze from my tightly closed eyes. My throat's so tight, I barely manage to get out:

"Both of them?"

"Yes, both of them. I'm sorry, Warren."

I've been worried about my right foot ever since I noticed the green spots on it. The possibility of losing it entered my mind then. But I pushed the thought away, not wanting to dwell on it. But the idea of losing more than the foot, in fact, both legs . . .

Both of them. Both my legs!

Tears stream down my face—not because I am thinking of what it will mean physically, how it will handicap me, turn me into a cripple. But because of the sheer loss. I can't imagine them not being there. My toes, my feet, my legs have always just been there. The terrible loss, of losing part of myself, tears at me like the pain of losing a loved one.

Struggling to get my words out, not knowing whether I want to hear an answer: "How high?"

"Fairly high, Warren. Above your knees."

No! Fuck, no! I cry out inside, an icy chill running through my core. "When?"

"We need to operate as soon as possible, tonight," is his reply.

No! Jeeeeeesus Christ!

"Is there anything else you can do? Can't you wait to see if they recover?"

"If we wait, Warren, for some kind of improvement, I'm afraid I don't think you will survive the night. Of course, we need your permission to carry out the operation. But it's my personal and professional opinion that if we don't carry out the operation tonight, there's a very real chance you won't survive the night."

My head feels like it's being squeezed from all sides, the pressure trying to compress my brain. I feel like I'm bracing myself for what I have to say.

"All right. Just do what you have to do."

The words drain me completely, as if part of my spirit has gone with them. I sign the permission form for the operation with tears coursing down my face.

Lying there naked under all those lights, I begin to retreat into myself: searching for strength, crying, feeling a sadness like I've never felt before. I can't begin to imagine the realm into which I'm headed, to comprehend what lies in front of me. I've never even had an operation before. I can't imagine my legs being cut.

Will it hurt? Will I die?

The magnitude of the situation overwhelms me.

I'm totally closed off from everything happening around me now, like I'm in some kind of tunnel or a room full of mirrors. Everything else is irrelevant as I cry myself to sleep, knowing I'm embarking on a journey into total darkness—and that, if I do come out, things can never be the same again.

By 2:30 AM on Saturday morning, both of my legs have been amputated at mid-thigh.

ABOVE: Using a self-timer, I took this shot in the prehistoric atmosphere of the Ruwenzori Mountains, the so-called "Mountains of the Moon" bordering Uganda and Zaire. *Photo Warren Macdonald*

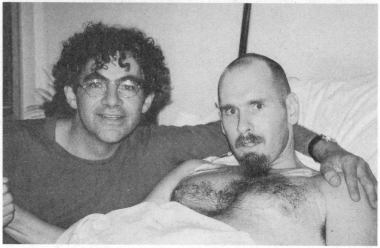

TOP: The scene greeting paramedic Chip Jaffurs as he reaches me in fading light. Hinchinbrook Island, April 11, 1997. *Photo Chip Jaffurs*

BOTTOM: With Geert van Keulen in Cairns Base Hospital, early May 1997. Note the morphine-induced "Charles Manson" look. *Photo Graeme Macdonald*

TOP LEFT: Walking for the first time outside hospital in the backyard at Mom and Dad's in December 1997. *Photo Graeme Macdonald*

TOP RIGHT: Celebrating after the Lorne "Pier to Pub" open water swim, January 10, 1998. *Photo Daphne Smith*

BOTTOM: Sanding back a bench seat for painting at Mom and Dad's. Simple jobs like this helped me realize that I had lost a hell of a lot, but not everything. *Photo Graeme Macdonald*

TOP: Gaining altitude the hard way. Cradle Mountain. *Photo Jeremy Smith*
BOTTOM: Sunset on the summit of Cradle Mountain, January 31, 1998.
From left: Eddie Storace, Ian Matthews, and myself. *Photo Cate Weate*

PART II

THE WILL
TO LIVE

You are a child of the universe, no less than the trees and

the stars . . . With all its sham, drudgery and broken

dreams, it is still a beautiful world.

DESIDERATA

A World Away

It was 10 PM on a quiet Friday night when the telephone rang in the Macdonald household, 3,500 kilometers (2,200 miles) from Cairns, in the western suburbs of Melbourne. Lisa, the youngest of four siblings, took the call, and her heart sank as the caller identified herself. Numb with shock, she went back into the living room. Her mother, Patricia, immediately sensed something terrible had happened and cried out in anguish, "Who is it love?"

"It's someone from the Cairns hospital. She wants to talk to Dad," she managed to utter before bawling, "Something's happened to Warren!"

Graeme Macdonald picked up the kitchen telephone, bracing himself for the worst as Dr. Katherine Swanson explained to him that his son Warren had been gravely injured in an accident. His son was about to go into surgery, where he would undergo the amputation of both his legs.

Graeme and Pat flew to Cairns on the next available flight, arriving at the hospital at 11:15 AM on Saturday morning. After being briefed by a social worker, they then met with Dr. John Morgan, an intensive care specialist based at the Royal Brisbane Hospital, who was in Cairns on a locum. He explained the seriousness of their son's condition.

"We think that he'll make it," Morgan said, before adding gravely: "But there is a chance he may die."

Thirty minutes later, they walked into their eldest son's new life.

Saturday Morning

Almost like being grabbed and pulled up hard from beneath a murky sea, I wake, feeling like a flashlight has been shoved in my face in the middle of the night. Terror grips me as I realize I'm choking. I try to cry out but can't.

Something's caught in my throat! I can't breathe!

I try to lift my arms, but they move in slow motion, as if they are still under the water.

What the hell's down my throat? It's choking me!

"Get this thing out of my throat! I can't breathe! Somebody help me!" I plead, but nothing more than a groan escapes my chest.

My sudden movements attract the attention of a nurse, and she's quickly beside me, trying to reassure me. "It's OK. You're all right. The tube is there to help you breathe. Just try to relax."

"It's choking me! It's fucking well choking me! Get it out! Please!"

Holding my arm, she keeps telling me I'm OK, but I try to struggle, my eyes widening, pleading for her to help me.

"Take it out, please! It's choking me!" I groan desperately.

Tears run down my face as I retch involuntarily, gagging on the plastic tube in my throat. Called an ET (endotracheal) tube, it has been pushed right down in my trachea to the point before the branches to my right and left lungs. Minutes pass. I'm still struggling, but I sense I can't take this thing out of my mouth, that it's there for a reason. As I slowly gain control over my throat convulsing, my discomfort is replaced by the pain that has lurked in the background for these first moments of my new life.

I feel like I've been hit by a truck. My whole body is racked with a heavy, dull ache, every bit of me sore and tight. I am sure that I'm going to burst out of my skin. There's no additional pain in my legs, they're just as sore as everything else. Actually, I'm not really thinking about them. I remember what happened, the events of the previous days are fresh in my mind. I know my legs are gone. Right at this moment, though, that's not my major concern. Overriding all else is one thought:

I am surely going to die.

The thought chills me inside. My stomach tightens and my entire body tenses as my breathing quickens in response to the realization. I can't believe I'm dying; I thought I'd been saved when I was rescued. But it's not over. The nurse is still beside me, reassuring me.

"It's OK. You're going to be OK. Just try to relax." As she speaks, her attention is focused on a monitor behind me. Occasionally she glances down, making sure I haven't pulled out any of the multitude of lines and wires attached to me. An immeasurable period of time passes. I'm amazed that she is the only one here, that there aren't more people here to save me. When I finally reach a point resembling "relaxed," she leans over and says, "There are some people here to see you."

Mom and Dad

Looking across the room, I see Mom and Dad moving toward me.

"Mom!" I whimper, unable to call out.

Reaching out, I take her hand and squeeze it tightly, tears streaming down both our faces.

"Oh, love," she manages to get out before closing her eyes in pain.

"Dad!"

Taking my other hand, "We're here, mate, it's all right," he says, voice breaking as the tears run down his face. I close my eyes, sobbing with relief that they are here with me.

Mom, still barely able to speak, squeezes my hand tighter and says, "I love you so much. You know that, don't you?"

I squeeze my eyes tight over burning tears and nod my head. *Yes, I do. I love you, too, Mom.*

I'm becoming distressed at being unable to speak, the frustration adding to my woes. I need to talk to them, to let them know how heartening it is to see them. I wish more than anything else they could just take this tube out so I can talk to them, rather than have me slip away like this in silence. Waves of despair flood over me, threatening to drown me.

Nooooooo! Don't let it happen like this! I need to . . . write. That's it.

I motion for a pen, eyes pleading for recognition. I feel a sense of urgency, as if I could go this very minute, and it makes me frantic in my actions. Dad recognizes immediately what I need and calls for the nurse, who reappears quickly with pen and paper. I have trouble holding the pen, my hands feel like they are inside thick gloves. I can hardly put pen to paper. When I finally do, all that results is scribble. Mom and Dad are trying to read it as I look on in utter frustration. I motion for the note back again, then try to write slowly this time, but it still comes out just a scribbled mess.

Noooooo! I scream inside with frustration.

One more try. Dad passes me the pad again and I slowly put the words together, using all my energy just to get them on the page:

"Good to see you."

"It's good to see you, too, love," Mom cries, Dad squeezing my hand.

Having them there has begun to lift me, and I feel like I have to fight back. I motion for the pad and pen, and Dad passes them back to me. With determination, I write:

"No fucking rock is going to beat me."

They both cry as they read it. I hold Mom's hand as I cry, too, face screwed up in anguish, hot tears squeezing from my eyes. It feels like this is the last time I'll ever see them, that we're saying goodbye. I realize this could be my last chance to let them both know how I really feel—what I have never said, what most of us have probably never said.

Then I remember. *My red book! They've got to read my journal!*

Dad passes me the pad again, sensing my urgency. Slowly and deliberately, I write:

"Red book."

Dad reads aloud, "Red book," looking to me for confirmation. I nod, squeezing my eyes shut with relief.

"Where is it mate?" he asks, and for a second I feel lost again.

I motion for the pad again and write, painfully slowly:

"Plastic bag."

I don't really know where it is. They might not even have brought it out with me. One of the rescue crew asked me, as they lifted me onto the stretcher before flying out of Warrawilla Creek, whether any of my belongings were family heirlooms.

"If you don't absolutely need it, we're going to have to leave it here," he said. My diary may have been left behind and been washed down the creek by now. They may never get to read it.

"It's OK, mate. We'll find it," Dad reassures me. I try to form words, but again they just come out in a groan as I try to emphasize the importance of finding that book. I feel myself slipping off, my energy drained from sheer emotion.

They've got to read it! is all that fills my mind as I drift off into an unknown time and space.

Only now, in hindsight, can I even begin to imagine what they must have been going through to see me like that: their eldest son horribly disfigured, barely alive.

Awakening

The next time I wake, it seems late at night. It's very quiet, and at first I think I'm alone. The tube is gone from my throat! Relief sweeps over me. I'm not choking any more. All I can think about is how thirsty I am; my throat feels so dry, it's like cardboard. I still can't think about what's happened. My mind is being occupied by other things, like thirst and pain. Seemingly from nowhere, a nurse appears at my side.

"How are you feeling?" she asks.

"OK, I think," I respond dryly.

"Can I get you anything?" she asks.

"I need something to drink, my throat's so dry," I reply in a hoarse whisper.

"What would you like?"

"What have you got?" I ask.

"We've got some cold water or some cordial."

"Have you got anything fizzy?" I ask, thinking I might be asking a bit much.

"Yeah, I could probably find you something in the kitchen. What would you like?"

"A can of Coke?" I ask hopefully, surprising myself as soon as the words leave my lips. I don't usually drink Coke.

"I think I may be able to dig some up for you," she smiles, and leaves the room. I don't think I've ever anticipated a mere drink so much before. I haven't had any fluids pass my lips since Friday afternoon. It is now somewhere around 8 PM, Saturday night. I am so thirsty!

The nurse returns with an icy cold can and pops a straw into it before handing it to me, though she's still holding onto it to save me from spilling any. I suck at it greedily, almost too quickly, and she stops me from drinking too much. The feeling, as thousands of tiny bubbles explode over my tongue, is like heaven. With incredible satisfaction, totally refreshed, I close my eyes and drift back into the hazy realm of a deep, dreamless sleep. (I wish now, years later, I could remember what my mind could possibly have been dreaming at that time, hovering between life and death. But I draw a blank. I was doped up on a combination of Fentanyl, a powerful narcotic, and Midazolam. Midazolam is a sedative, similar in effect to Valium. A standard dose of five milligrams two to three times per day produces an amnesic effect. I was on five milligrams per hour.)

I AWAKE to find a number of people talking at the foot of my bed, one of whom introduces himself as Dr. John Morgan.

"So, how are we feeling?" he asks.

"All right," comes my reply. (The drugs are obviously working.)

"You're a lucky man. You must be a strong bugger to still be with us, you know."

"I don't know about that," I reply, not feeling that lucky.

"Do you understand what's happened to you?" he asks seriously.

"Yeah, I think so," I answer, hoping there is no more to know than the obvious.

"We have had to amputate both your legs," he begins. "They were very badly damaged and couldn't be saved."

I nod in reply, my throat tightening at hearing it said for the first time since the surgery. Nobody has mentioned my legs up until now. I feel like I am fighting for my life and that my legs are the least of my worries.

"We have left the wounds open, Warren, so we can monitor them for a few days. Once we can be sure there's no infection, we'll close the wounds."

"OK" is all I can say. *So it's not over, I've got to have another operation.*

All this attention on my legs is forcing me to finally confront my new reality. I'm trying to comprehend that they're gone, that the wounds have not been closed. I picture the ends, open and bloody, flaps of skin draped over them. The thought turns my stomach. *God, I hope they close them up soon.*

Dr. Morgan explains that I also have a hairline fracture of my pelvis, from the rock's initial impact, I presume. He then briefs the nurse beside him before leaving. I go back to floating in my sea of unreality, unaware of any pain, with just the bizarre feeling that my feet have been squashed. It's like they've been squeezed into a pair of shoes that are much too small, and they feel really cold and numb. Looking down my body to the empty space under the sheets, I consciously have to push the rising thoughts out of my head. *Don't, mate. Don't even think about it. Not yet.*

I drift off into the sanctuary of sleep, only to be awoken a short time later by the nurse. "You've got some visitors. Would you like to see them?" she asks.

"Yes, who is it?" I answer, looking toward the door as Mom and Dad walk in, my question answered.

"How are you, love?" asks Mom, holding my hand and leaning down to hug me gently. "I'm all right," I manage to get out, my eyes holding back tears. "G'day Dad," and I reach out my hand to take his.

"Did you find it?" I ask, my voice strained with emotion. "Did you find the book?"

"Yes, mate. We found it," says Dad, squeezing my hand tighter.

"Did you read it?" The tears are threatening to squeeze out.

"We did, love," Mom replies, leaning down to hug me again, eyes welling.

"That was the hardest thing I've ever had to do," she cries. I hold her tight, trying to imagine how it must have been for her to read. Knowing that, as I wrote those entries, I fully expected to die—that those were, in fact, my last words.

"I love you, Warren," she sobs into my shoulder.

"I love you, too, Mom," I cry, holding her tightly, hot tears streaming down my face. We hold each other for some time before Mom breaks the silence.

"There's someone else here to see you, love. Lisa flew up this morning. Would you like to see her?"

"Yeah, I would," I reply, my joy mixed with uneasiness at my sister seeing me like this. I've always been her big brother. We have always been close, the youngest and the oldest, and I fear how she may perceive me now.

When she walks into the room and comes toward me, tears filling her eyes, I lose it again. Taking my hand and leaning down to me, she cries into my shoulder, "I love you, Wogsy" (her nickname for me since we were kids).

"I love you too, Lee," I sob as I hold her tight, choking with emotion. It is so good to see her. I haven't seen any of my family since flying down to Melbourne for Dirk and Sharon's wedding, back in February. Seeing Lisa again now, after what I've been through, I feel as if I've been given a second chance. I vow to spend more time with my family.

Acceptance

I spend the next ten days in the intensive care ward. I feel as if I'm in some kind of suspended animation, time swirling around me like a fog. At times, I feel no pain at all. Other times, I ache all over, a deep ache that seems to penetrate my bones. And my skin still feels incredibly tight, stretched over my swollen body, squeezing me.

I feel completely drained, possibly because I'm still losing almost 2 liters (2 quarts) of blood per day. The blood is being continuously replaced through my IV line, and the nurse repeatedly changes the bags hanging on the stand beside me. In fact, by the end of my stay in intensive care, I'll have received more than 15 liters/3.5 gallons (35 units of packed red blood cells at 330 ml per unit; 30 units of platelets—the clotting mechanism of blood—at 70 ml per unit, and 10 units of fresh frozen plasma at 150 ml per unit). The average person has 6.5 liters (1.5 gallons) of blood in their entire body.

Within a few days of the initial operation, anxious friends are calling the hospital. At times, talking to them gives me enormous strength. And sometimes, when I can't see any way out, it just makes me feel worse. At these times, I decline to talk and ask the nurses to tell the caller I'm OK, or I get Mom or Dad to speak to them if it's someone they know. Messages and cards offering best wishes and support also come flooding in, and I'm often moved to tears by friends putting feelings that are rarely expressed into words.

When the call comes through from Geert, I take the telephone anxiously. I had almost forgotten about him, my thoughts occupied somewhat. But I need to thank him. I want to hear his story of getting down the mountain and let him know I'm OK.

He's calling from Townsville, where he's staying with friends, trying to rest and take in what has happened. He tells me how a television helicopter gave him a ride off the island. I reassure him that I'm OK, that my family are with me now. I'm not prepared for his next question, though.

"How are your legs, mate. Were they broken?" My stomach churns with the realization. *He doesn't know!*

"Didn't they tell you?"

"Tell me what?" he asks, concern filling his voice.

I swallow hard before answering, "They had to cut them off, mate."

A stony silence fills the line, neither of us speaking for what seems like an eternity.

"Christ, Warren. I don't know what to say," he says finally, his voice a hollow shell for the words.

"It's all right. You did everything you could." My voice is strained. "You got me out of there. You saved my life."

Silence takes over again, the kind of silence that says more than words. "Can I come up and see you, Warren?"

"Yeah, mate. That'd be good."

On Wednesday, the rest of my family flies up from Melbourne to see me. Michelle comes in first. As we hold each other, tears streaming down her face, I think of how she must feel. Michelle is a nurse; medically she must know how bad it is, how bad it was from the start. She must have witnessed this scenario a hundred times from the relative comfort of the sidelines.

I go through the same apprehension with the rest of the family that I went through with Lisa, especially with Matty, my six-year-old nephew. When my brother Brett walks into the room with him, Matthew looks anxiously at the space under the covers where my legs are supposed to be, then ducks down to see if he can see them hanging beneath the bed. He must be thinking it's some kind of magic trick. The concept of someone's legs being cut off is probably too strange for him to come to grips with. He keeps his distance from me, almost as if he is too scared to come close. It's my first experience of the way kids will respond when they see me now. I scare them, and it's a feeling I think I'll never get used to.

Seeing my family again totally drains me. Such intense emotions are being dragged to the surface, ranging from pure joy at being alive and able to be with them, to fear and doubt over their acceptance of me. It's a fear I won't really be able to explain until some twelve months from now, when I see a TV documentary set in Africa. There's a particular scene in the film that captures my fear, a scene that's set around a rapidly diminishing water hole, left behind after the river has ceased to flow at the onset of the dry season. The only source of water left in the area for all the animals, it becomes the focal point for their survival. However, through a cruel twist of fate, it is full of crocodiles. And they're massed together in what becomes no more than a mud slurry, lying in wait for the next thirsty baboon or impala to take their chance and venture forward for a drink.

As the mud hole evaporates, shrinking in size bit by bit, it becomes a seething pit. Writhing and rolling, the crocodiles fight amongst themselves over the carcasses of the victims so far. Nothing but a few boggy holes, mainly hoof prints filled with water, remain near the edge. But even these are within the crocs' reach, and any animal that ventures forward to drink is dragged into the pit.

An atmosphere of madness begins to take hold. It's an insanity wrought from the absolute helplessness, the cruelty of the situation— like a scene set in hell, where there is no happy ending, only prolonged pain and suffering. One by one, the animals are drawn to the water through desperation, then quickly torn apart by the waiting crocs.

Eventually, a young baboon ambles to the edge, having decided, I suppose, that it is better to risk dying in an attempt to drink than to die slowly of thirst under the hot sun. But as he bends down, a huge croc leaps forward and seizes him by the head. The baboon, squealing in terror, has both hands on the croc's jaws, trying to pry them open, to pull his head out of the vice-like jaws. For what seems like an agonizing eternity, he's held there on the bank, until, miraculously, he breaks free. Scampering away, bleeding from deep gashes to his head, the baboon looks terrified. He stops at the top of the bank and looks frantically around with haunted eyes, desperate for some kind of support, some comfort.

All he is met with are stares. The other baboons look upon him as a ghost, as if he shouldn't be alive, not after that. They're scared of him, scared of what he's been through. Why? Is it because he has forced them to face their own mortality?

Why is it that we are frightened of people who have been to the edge? I ask myself. Is it because they have glimpsed the other side and we don't want to contemplate what they have seen, opting instead for blissful ignorance?

Watching that film, never have I felt so much pity for another being as I did for the baboon standing there alone, desperately needing someone to go to him, to hold him, to comfort him. But nobody came. He was no longer one of them.

The Surgery Never Stops

During the ten days I spend in intensive care, I go into surgery another five times. Most of the early operations involve the debridement of necrotic tissue, but one, only four days after my initial surgery, results in my right femur being shortened a further 4 centimeters (2 inches) due to an infection that has crept up the bone. Dr. Morgan had been concerned about the smell coming from one of my stumps, the smell of rotting flesh. I didn't even notice it until he mentioned it, and I suppose nobody else was game to say anything. "Gee, your legs stink!" I don't think so. I was impressed to see a doctor using a skill as basic and down to earth as his sense of smell to make a diagnosis. When a patient's wounds reek like a bag of prawns left out in the sun, there's really no need to sit around and wait for lab results.

I dread the occasions when Dr. Morgan comes to check on me, sniffing around my dressings. I know that if they don't smell good, I'll be off to the operating theater again. The thought of further operations terrifies me, and not just because of my fear of being cut open while asleep—that alone is bad enough. But what scares me more is that, each time they operate, they take another piece of me away.

Surely I can't lose any more of my legs! Haven't I lost enough already?

Each time the rotting smell raises its head again, I go into a deep depression, praying for an end to this so I can start to recover. I feel like I'm not actually getting anywhere, like I'm hanging in the balance, still capable of going either way. And every time I go into surgery, I come out so drained that I feel like I'm back to square one.

I can't think beyond the present, can't picture life beyond the room I'm in. All I can focus on is getting better, and that depresses me more than anything because it's beyond my control. My legs are still plagued by infection. I pray each time I wake after surgery or Dr. Morgan enters the room on his ward round that it's over, that there'll be no more surgery, that they have finally cut out all the infection and can now leave me alone. Only then will I be able to regain control, be back in charge of my life. In the meantime, all I can do for myself is keep my sanity—by totally blocking out what has happened to me. I'm in no fit state to deal with reality right now. There'll be plenty of time for that later.

Time becomes meaningless as I go from recovering from one operation to being prepared for the next, seemingly with no breaks in between. Before each operation, the dreaded "Nil by mouth" sign is hung on the end of my bed. For eight hours prior, I'm allowed no food or drink to ensure an empty stomach in the operating room. The food part I don't have a problem with. I have no appetite at this stage, anyway. But the lack of fluid I find unbearable. I've been so thirsty ever since waking up. I just can't seem to get enough fluid into me, and not being able to drink almost sends me around the bend. I beg the nurses to at least give me one of their foul-tasting, popsicle-like, lemon-glycerin swab sticks. Sucking them makes me feel like I'm getting *some* fluid. I'm even beginning to like them, which is a bit of a worry.

Having two of my closest friends come to visit lifts my spirits enormously—just knowing they're here, that they care enough to be with
me when I need them most. Belinda Wells flies all the way from Melbourne, and Natalie Dudding, who is like a third sister to me, catches
the train up from Brisbane. I can't imagine what it's like for them to see
me as I am, but I'm glad they have the courage to walk into my room. I
only wish they could both be here at the same time so they can finally
meet, but they miss each other by a matter of days.

Belinda and Natalie, along with Mom and Dad, come by to see me
every day of their respective visits, bringing me freshly squeezed juice
and anything else I need. Mom and Dad move out of the motel they've
been staying in, invited by friends Paul and Karen Wilson to share their
nearby home. An airline pilot, Graham Bigby (known to Dad through
his work as a maintenance specialist with Qantas) has given them the
use of his car.

I feel guilty that I've spent so much time away from my family. I wonder now whether it has been selfishness on my part. I hope they have understood what has driven me, the constant quest for adventure, the
search for meaning. It is always so good to see them again after I've been
away for a while. They give me a sense of stability. But before too long, I
always find myself feeling anxious again—as if I'm missing out on something by sitting back in comfortable surroundings rather than being out
there, at the frontier. For me, it seems, life is not something to be experienced from a living room chair. I feel agitated if I'm not challenging myself in some way. I'm also not worth being around when I feel caught in a
rut, so at those times I don't like to inflict myself on other people. But
I'm learning, through having Mom and Dad up here with me now, that
they'll always support me in whatever I do, as long as I'm happy.

THE HOSPITAL'S physiotherapist has given me an instrument she
wants me to use called a Triflow—a clear plastic pipe-like gadget housing three hollow balls. I have to blow into it and try and keep all three
balls suspended as long as possible on a cushion of air. This is to keep
my lungs active and prevent them from holding fluid. Apparently this is

a big problem when someone is immobilized for any length of time, and can lead to pneumonia. I become obsessed with the gadget and use it at every opportunity. I recognize this as my first active step, the first part for me to play in my own recovery.

GEERT VAN KEULEN: *Reunion*

THE MORNING AFTER the accident, I discovered my ragged face on the cover of the state's newspaper.

"Desperate Hike Saves Companion" the headline read, and I smiled and bought five copies to mail home. After reading the article, I then called the hospital. I explained who I was, and the nurse told me I could talk to Warren directly by cellphone. That's what we should have had up there, I thought—a cellphone!

I spoke to Warren, who was very doped up. But he managed to thank me, then calmly told me that he had lost both of his legs. I couldn't believe it. I asked him to repeat the words, which he did. I felt sad, through and through, and very angry. Never in my imagination did I envisage Warren without legs. Of course, it made sense. His circulation had been cut off for such a long time. He had been trapped for forty-six hours. But the news shocked me. I felt like someone who has lost a dear friend or relative and can't believe that the person is gone. In anger, I ran from Rohan's bedroom and cried. I felt responsible and guilty for the accident; it was I who had asked him to come along with me. Rohan calmed me down as he tried to talk some sense into me.

At 6 PM, WIN television broadcast the story. It was the main news item. The station showed the accident site from the air, the rescuers working on Warren with tools and equipment, and the interview with me on the beach. Rohan videotaped the entire segment. (Much later, when I was back in the safety of my own living room in the Netherlands, watching it again would help me a great deal to overcome my trauma, and to remember vital moments and the landscape of the island.)

The days following were spent relaxing, as I tried to get my adrenaline level down (which just didn't happen). For days I could not sleep properly, nor unwind. The headaches got worse. But at Rohan and

Trish's place, I had found the perfect shelter. I called my girlfriend and parents and explained what had happened, and that I wanted to recuperate more before heading home. And when I felt ready, I decided to visit Warren. I wasn't sure whether he would want to see me or even whether he could, so I called the hospital first and spoke to a nurse who said it would be important for me to come down. On the Thursday after Warren's rescue, I boarded a bus in Townsville and headed for Cairns, a six-hour trip.

On arrival, I was snatched by two social workers who knew about my visit. For about half an hour, we talked about the accident, they then gave me a pile of articles on how to deal with trauma. "Survivor guilt," they called the symptoms I was showing. Then I sterilized my hands and was allowed on the intensive care ward, where I met one of Warren's sisters, Michelle. She cried a little and hugged me, and thanked me for what I'd done. I felt quite overwhelmed and uneasy.

Warren lay in a mess of wires, computers, monitors, and LED lights, breathing heavily through an oxygen mask, which he was fighting. He had just come out of surgery and was in a morphine-induced state of narcosis. I looked at him. Where I expected his legs was a sheet and a white blanket. Half a human being. His thighs were slightly splayed and covered by a thick layer of bandages. His legs had been removed to about 10 or 15 centimeters (4 or 6 inches) above his knees, one left a bit longer than the other. Every few minutes, a little alarm would go off and a nurse would come by to change a drip or check on the equipment around him.

The social workers watched how I approached Warren, then left me with him. I stroked his forehead and looked at his face. His small, ginger-colored beard was tightened to his chin because of the mask. I looked around the room. The hospital was in an old building. In contrast with a lot of the surrounding buildings in Cairns, this place was in financial need. The apparatus and equipment, however, seemed modern, as far as I could judge. And the wall next to Warren was covered with yellow Post-it Notes carrying a load of get well wishes from friends all over Australia. A few postcards had already made it to the hospital, too. My address and telephone number in Townsville were also pinned on the wall.

I whispered a few words to him, and his eyes opened a little and slowly scanned the room. When they met mine, he said, "Thank you, mate. I didn't think you'd make it." I knew he meant the hike down the mountain, not the trip to the hospital. After that he fell silent. There wasn't much to talk about at that stage, and I sat down on a stool by his bed. I felt relieved, tired, and humble.

"Another job done," I thought to myself. I had really worked myself up for the visit. I knew I had to see Warren, and there was no way I wouldn't have done it, but I felt very uneasy about it. Meeting his parents and other relatives was going to be another difficult part of the visit. But now, my deep tiredness manifested itself for the first time since the accident. The adrenaline had not stopped pumping until now. I yawned, then watched as Warren slowly came out of the narcosis, his big, strong shoulders, chest, and arms showing above the white bed linen, wires and tubes connected to them, and I marvelled at his sense of humor and strong will to live as I found myself wondering, "What if this accident had happened to me...?"

Noise in the corridor roused me out of my daydream, and suddently his parents were in front of me. His mother hugged me and cried, and his dad said, "How can I ever thank you?" I must have mumbled something, but I can't remember what. I had imagined that they would be very angry with me for taking Warren on the hike, but instead, I was given respect and gratitude. I did not feel like I deserved it. The guilt was too strong.

Later, during my visit, three members of the QES rescue chopper crew crowded in: the pilot, winchman, and a crewman. Obviously, it wasn't the first time they had checked in on Warren. The winchman asked if I had built the back support that they found Warren in. I said "Yes," and he explained that building the chair had saved Warren's life. Had he been lying down, his lungs would have not been able to cope and he would have died. I hadn't realized that it would be so important. My aim had been only to give him a little comfort. But it was good to hear and it relaxed me a little. The crewman also asked if I was all right. "Yeah," I replied, and thanked them all for what they had done for Warren. One of them made a joke about my appearance at the beach; saying, "Well, you finally had a shave!"—to which Warren added from beneath his oxygen mask, "Yeah, he's a bit of a wild man. A wild man from Borneo!" After that, he drifted away once more.

Around 5 PM, I left Warren behind in his Star Wars room full of monitors, tubes, and drips, and walked on the streets of Cairns. When I arrived back at the hospital at 8 PM, Warren was being transferred from intensive care to the coronary ward. This gave him more space and quiet, as he was the only patient on the ward. There I met a charming friend of Warren's who'd come all the way from Brisbane by train (a thirty-two-hour trip) to be with him—Natalie, from New Zealand. The three of us chatted for a while. Warren was once again trying to be funny. I showed him the sketches of the accident that I had drawn from memory, but realized that I'd been premature in hoping we could talk about it. He had other things on his mind. I had made photocopies of the drawings, my notes, and a few newspaper articles that I'd gathered and I left those with him. I was sure one day he would, or could, use them.

At 10 PM, Natalie and I left and walked into the tropical Cairns night, and, over a drink, she listened to my story. The gratitude and support I received from her were good to experience. But at 11 PM, when I hit the sack in the hostel, I was again plagued by my usual burning headache, from the top of my head to behind my eyes, then to my teeth and down below my shoulders. Fortunately it didn't prevent me from falling asleep. The next morning, I went back to the hospital at 11 AM and found Warren in the company of his parents and Natalie. He was happy to see me. I saw a spark in his eyes that wasn't there the day before. And I thought of how, immediately after I heard that he'd lost his legs, I wondered if he would want to live, being such a fit man and now suddenly an invalid. But now, I was only happy that he was still alive.

After talking to him and his parents for a while, Natalie and I went for another walk. We lunched at the art gallery, then sat down on a bench looking at the mudflats, where I sketched the scene as we chatted. Together we went through the history of the past couple of days. Of course, it had come to her as a shock, too, and she had not been able to rest until she got on the train to come up here. She told me that Warren had been in critical shape on the Tuesday, three days before. His mother had already told me that even she had thought Warren would not see the end of that day; his face was so swollen, his attitude lethargic. But on the next day, things began to look up. Natalie then told me about some of the peculiarities in Warren's character and praised his sense of humor. We discussed the use of meditation and rest, talking quietly until it was time for another visit. This time I saw Warren for only five minutes. He was very tired and needed all the rest he could get.

Natalie and I joined the Macdonald family for dinner that night, and they made me feel like I was, for that occasion at least, one of them. At their encouragement, I ate an enormous sirloin steak garnished with pepper sauce. It barely fit on my plate—the Queensland way. As I drank three glasses of South Australian Cooper's ale, Warren kept coming up in the conversation. Everyone was eager to listen to my side of the adventure, too. But the conversation was never sad. We were all very relieved and happy that Warren was still amongst us.

Diary: Saturday, April 19, 1997 I'm sitting outside a coffee shop somewhere in Cairns: Mozart's. The place is packed with bungee jumpers, reef divers and snorkellers, paintballers, and whitewater rafters. A lot of money is being circulated in this town—Japanese and Western. The laid-back atmosphere that it had fourteen years ago has gone. This is my last day here and it's all been a bit much for me, I realize, as I'm yearning for peace and quiet. But first, I still have a little work to do. I plan to walk to the local library and browse through the newspapers from the past week, then photocopy the items that carry information about the accident. Both the environmentalists and the pro-development politicians wrestling over Hinchinbrook Island have jumped on Warren's bandwagon, trying to steal the limelight to push their causes. I will put the copies in an envelope and add them to the sketches in Warren's bedside drawer. I think he will want to have this information when he's on the road to recovery back in Melbourne. He's probably being operated upon at this very moment....

After a telephone call to the hospital, I learn that Warren is being "opened up" again at 1 PM.

THE VISIT to Warren in the afternoon was a long one. I arrived at 2 PM, and sat with him for an hour and a half. I asked permission from the nurse to sketch him, and when he came out of his narcosis, she relayed my question to him and he agreed. So I studied him and drew his face. I was the only visitor. A thick furrow across his forehead showed that he was involved in yet another battle. He was very quiet and, even after he had come out of it, his mood seemed the lowest I'd seen so far. We didn't talk much. I was happy and content to be with him, alone in this large, quiet room. Although slowly, my contentment gave way to the reality of Warren's fate. I started to look at him differently as the time passed, and I confronted myself with my "I'm sitting in his way" attitude. Luckily Pat and Graeme Macdonald came to my rescue when they walked in shortly afterward.

Warren's favorite drink was apple, carrot, and celery fruit juice, which his parents usually bought for him from a shop in town. This was a good opportunity for me to go and get one for him. And it gave Warren and his parents some privacy. But the shop had run out of apples, and with no juice I returned to the hospital, where it seemed he had overcome his depression and was fighting for his new life once again. At 5:30 PM, I said my goodbyes. It was a difficult moment.

"I'll see you later, Warren." I hugged him and walked into the corridor where four family members were waiting to go in. I said goodbye to them as well, then met Warren's parents outside on the lawn, where I said goodbye again.

ON MAY 2, my flight back to Europe would depart from Cairns airport. And in those last few weeks, I tried to get loose from the accident. I ate well and was spoiled by Trish, swam within the protection of the stinger nets off the Townsville beach, and discussed my plans for the future. Slowly, my insomnia eased, and I began to recuperate and to feel ready to go home. I called the hospital in Cairns on the chance that Warren was still there. I expected that he had been transferred to Melbourne, but to my surprise and delight he hadn't yet left.

On the day of my departure, for the last time I took the bus to Cairns, through the sugar cane fields of North Queensland. At the hospital I found a sparkling Warren, with his happier and much more relaxed parents. He looked so much better and talked a lot. Much of his wiring and tubing were gone, and above his bed there was a construction from which he could pull himself up. It was fantastic to see him that way, full of spirit. What a strong individual he is. Graeme took a photograph of us, a nice moment, as Warren strongly held my hands. Then they left to give us some privacy. We talked about his experiences up on the mountain, about the black ants in his groin, the noise of the water, the weather, the yabby story—and the phantom pains he still felt.

Then I said goodbye for the last time (for the near future, anyway) and walked out of the hospital to where Pat and Graeme were waiting for me. Together we walked to the Esplanade, where we drank a cup of coffee. When they dropped me off at my guesthouse, I said my final goodbyes to these kind people, too. When would I see Warren again? I knew that I would be back one day.

Fever, Pain, and Nightmares

My legs are far from the only casualty of the accident. Alhough most of the rock's weight was taken by my legs, a significant amount of it rested in my lap. And for a while at least, the pain in my legs is taking a back seat to what I'm experiencing between them.

The pain is excruciating. My testicles have swollen to the size of oranges, stretching my scrotum to the point where I thought it might split. But it has held firm and, in doing so, is pushing my now enormous testes back into me. No amount of painkillers can do anything to stem the pain. I seriously want the surgeons to cut them out and put them back in when the swelling goes down. *Surely they can do that. This is the nineties, for God's sake!*

I feel like I need to lie on my side in the fetal position to relieve the pain, but can't. My fractured pelvis prevents me from lying in any position except on my back. I lie here, praying for sleep to take me away from the pain, but it never comes when I really need it. Sweat rolls off me as I tense from side to side, trying to relieve the pressure. A fever has me sweating so much through the night that my sheets have to be changed regularly, sometimes at 3 or 4 AM. I feel as though I'm fighting a losing battle, and wonder if this whole thing could possibly get any worse.

From intensive care, I'm moved temporarily into the coronary unit until a bed becomes free in the general ward. Lying on my stomach for the first time, I fall asleep, but awake in a fright to the sounds of raised voices. An old Italian man in the bed diagonally opposite me has a couple of visitors, and they're in a heated argument. Their voices are growing louder and more aggravated, until I don't want to look over there in case they think I'm interfering. Sensing something is very wrong, I look over, to see one of them holding to the old man's throat what appears to be a knife. I freeze in terror.

What the hell's going on? This can't be happening?

I look again, turning my head just slightly, and squeeze my eyes tightly shut at the confirmation. I want to call out but can't. Never have I felt so utterly vulnerable, so helpless as I do at this moment. Lying on my stomach, I can't defend myself in even the feeblest way. I can't even roll over without help! If I call out, surely they'll turn on me. I lie there, frozen, trembling inside as I tried to remain invisible, hoping they'll take no notice and leave me alone.

The argument continues between the two men, the old man fighting back at times, the knife still held to his throat, me almost holding my breath for fear of drawing any attention. At the sound of further commotion, I look up in horror to see my brother Brett walk into the room. I try to yell out to him but no sound comes. I recoil in horror as the man with the knife lunges toward him, grabbing him as he walks by, bringing the knife up to his throat.

"Brett! Nooooo!" I yell inside, no sound leaving my throat. "Leave him alone!"

Suddenly I'm wrenched back by someone's voice, one of the nurses. Startled, I turn quickly to the corner of the room, eyes wide with sheer terror. There is nobody there except the old man, looking very much alive. I'm delirious, racked with fear as I try to describe what I've just seen.

"Where's my brother? Is he all right? Where is he? There was a knife!" I ramble hysterically.

She puts her hand on my arm, trying to reassure me. "It's OK. He hasn't been in here. No one has. You've been having a bad dream."

"He was. I saw him. They had a knife!"

"It's OK. It's only a dream. He's all right," she continues, but I'm not having any of it.

"What if they come back! I've seen them, they'll come back for me!" I cry.

"No they won't. There hasn't been anyone here. You've been having a bad dream."

"I can't stay here! You've got to get me out! Get me out of here!" I plead.

I stay terrified, almost frantic, until finally, after five milligrams of Valium, I begin to relax and drift off into the relative sanctuary of sleep. *Or do I?* I don't know how much later it is when I wake again, but I quickly recall what happened earlier and can't believe I'm still here, in the same room.

But it's not just that I'm in the same room. I'm alone.

I'm still here. No! I've got to get out. They're going to come back for me!

Looking around the dark, empty room, my gaze falls on a sectioned off area behind a drawn curtain. *They could be hiding in there!* I try not to look over, try to put the whole thing out of my mind, but it's useless. I've only just decided to call out for the nurse when I sense that someone is watching me. I try not to look but can't avert my eyes before they settle on the dark shadow in the folds of the curtain.

My heart skips a beat at the sight of a dark face, clearly visible, peering at me from the shadows.

No! Leave me alone! What are you doing here?

I try not to stare, terrified to let him know I see him. I squeeze my eyes shut and pray this isn't happening. There's no one here. *There can't be, can there?* Opening one eye ever so slightly, like you do when you're pretending you're asleep, I look again. I can barely contain my sharp intake of breath, then I hold it there as the ball of fear in my stomach tightens. He's there all right, staring straight back at me! I'm already terrified, but what happens next is too much. The shadowed features that I'm desperately trying to convince myself can't possibly be a face, slowly, and without question, blink.

I can't move, can't even think any more. I've ceased to exist, can't afford to exist while I lie vulnerable to whatever the intruder has in mind. Time stands still, the very air, the very fabric of existence frozen with me. I lie like this for what might be minutes or perhaps hours, I'll never know, for the sound of someone entering the room brings me back.

"How are we going over here now, feeling better?" the nurse asks casually, unaware of the danger.

"No, I'm not," I manage to reply, my voice a thin whimper. "I've got to tell you something." I'm too scared to cry out, to tell her out loud what is happening, for fear of provoking *him*. She won't be able to stop him on her own, and when he's finished with her, it will be my turn.

"What is it?" she asks, sensing the fear in my voice. "What's the matter?"

"Please, come over here so I can tell you," I plead with her, so scared now that tears well in my eyes. She comes up to the side of my bed and leans down. "What is it, what's the matter?"

As quietly as I can, I whisper, "You've got to get help. There's somebody in here who wants to kill me."

Without flinching, she holds my arm reassuringly. "There's no one here going to hurt you, Warren. You've been having a bad dream."

Glancing past her, back toward the curtains, the menacing face glares straight back at me. I grip her arm and beg her, "You've got to get help. You've got to get out of here. He'll kill you too!" Tears run down my face.

"There's nobody here, Warren. I'll show you. Now, where did you say they were? Behind here?" She takes hold of the curtain to draw it back.

"Yes," I nod. "But don't do it! You need to get help!" I plead loudly, trying not to be heard from the other side of that curtain.

With that she draws it back quickly. I have to turn away.

"See. There's nothing there," she says, certain that this will convince me. But I'm sure he'll leap out at any moment from deeper within the room while she has her back turned, for she is still facing me and hasn't really looked inside.

"No, he's in there," I plead as she walks away, toward the door. "Nooooo! Don't leave me here! You've got to get me out!"

As I cry after her, I look back in terror to the partially exposed room behind the curtain, peering into the dark spaces and hidden corners that could still be hiding him, knowing he is still in there, waiting. I feel myself slip away again, unable to deal with being left alone when I thought I was saved, slipping, slipping into an icy void, surrounded by black.

Sleep offers me little sanctuary.

I wake up to the sounds of voices arguing in the corridor outside the ward. It sounds like my sister Michelle, yelling at someone; them yelling at her. Their voices become louder and louder until they are screaming at each other. "For Gods' sake, shut up! Stop arguing," I scream in my head as the voices get louder.

It sounds like more people are involved now, and the raised voices intensify into the sounds of a fight.

"Michelle, get out of here!" I scream in my head. "Get me out of here." I lie frozen solid as what sound like a full-scale riot erupts, first in the corridor outside then throughout the whole hospital. Windows are being smashed, doors being kicked in, people are running and screaming.

I lie completely still, too terrified to move. I feel completely helpless, totally at the mercy of anyone who might burst into the room. I retreat into myself, trying to pretend this isn't happening. I try to imagine myself escaping somehow and, in an instant, I'm pulling myself along on my stomach in a trench outside the hospital. I watch in horror as carloads of people pull up outside the hospital, throw rocks through the windows, and fight amongst themselves. *I hope Michelle got out of here,* is all I can think. *God, I hope no one else is in there!* I watch as the building catches fire and becomes an inferno. Sinking my face down into the dirt, I'm sobbing and shaking my head in denial, praying for some kind of release, for an end to the madness.

The halucinary dreams continue for another two long days and nights. Later, a doctor will explain that they were likely a side effect of the narcotics. In hindsight, I would have preferred to try and deal with the pain.

Retaliation

The thing that drives me on, more than anything else, is the need to regain control. For the first weeks, I can barely move at all and must be "rolled" manually each time my sheets need changing. The indignity of having to be turned over like this needs to be experienced to be understood. What makes the experience even more repellant is the incredible pain that radiates out from my broken pelvis every time I go through it. The nurses aren't permitted to do it themselves and have to call in ward staff, or "wardies," to do the rolling.

The majority of the staff taking care of me in Cairns treat me well. However, some of the wardies treat me like a bag of meat. Intent on getting back to another game of table tennis or their favorite soap opera, they flip me over like a side of beef while ignoring my pleas to take it easy. *I've got a broken pelvis, for Christ's sake!*

I dread the times when the nurse calls them to roll me, and begin looking for a way to make the wardies redundant. *I'm not having those bastards treat me like this any longer.*

My bed has an overhead frame—the type used for patients in traction. Looking up at the bar above my head, I conjure up a plan. If I can sit forward and reach up, I can just curl my fingers around it. *Right! That's it! You bastards are out of my life!*

I start reaching up and holding on to that bar whenever I can, for a little longer each time. Before long, I can raise myself slightly from the bed, but only for a few seconds. That's enough, though. The next time my sheets need changing and the nurse mentions calling the wardies, I tell her not to worry about it.

"I don't want them touching me again. We can do it this way." And reaching up for the bar, I lift myself off the sheets. I think she's impressed.

This single step forward gives me an incredible sense of satisfaction. I've regained some control—a small amount, maybe, but it's a huge step toward getting back some of the freedom that I value so much. The satisfaction of doing something for myself, of not having to rely on someone else, is tremendous. This single decision to regain control over one aspect of my life sets the pattern for the rest of my recovery.

OK, *let's do it. I want my life back!*

—— THAT'S MY MATE! ——

I've always been hard on myself, harder than anyone else can be. I get so disappointed if I do something stupid or weak, usually punishing myself verbally at least.

While working in a pub in London, England, for example, I got fairly drunk one night while having a few quiet drinks after work. I'd just caught the last train at the Waterloo station and was thanking my lucky stars, because I couldn't really afford the cab fare home. I took a seat and settled back for the short ride to Clapham Junction, two stops away.

"C'mon, don't go to sleep. It's only two stops," I told myself as my head slowly dropped toward my chest, only to jerk up suddenly when it got there. *Bloody hell! Five more minutes and you'll be there. Stay awake!*

My head snapped up, eyes wide as I realized I'd been asleep. *The station!* I jumped up and swung open the door, stepping out onto the platform as the train began moving again. That was lucky, I thought to myself, I nearly missed it. But my thoughts of good fortune sank like the *Titanic* as my blurry eyes focused on the sign above me: "Hounslow."

"How did I get to Hounslow? I only closed my eyes for a minute!" I mumbled angrily to myself. (It had been twenty-five minutes.)

Walking along the platform, I came to a timetable. *Time? What time is it now?* Hanging overhead was a huge digital clock, its green display declaring 01:45. I turned back to the timetable and scanned the rows and columns until they eventually told me what I already knew. I *had* been on the last train. *Shit! You bloody idiot! What are you going to do now?*

I was so angry with myself, spitting and cursing as I walked along the platform and out into the street. What made me even angrier was the fact that this wasn't the first time it had happened. The last time I'd ended up like this, it had cost me, £30 ($60) to catch a cab. *You're not doing that this time, mate! You're going to have to deal with it!*

I decided to find somewhere to sleep and catch the first train home in the morning. Wandering around a nearby mall, looking for a sheltered doorway to sleep in, I felt like a complete derelict. *You were stupid enough to do this again. You can put up with it!* I tried lying down on some cardboard boxes behind a pizza shop, but a cold wind had got there first and swirled around me, making sleep impossible.

"God, it's cold!" I said out loud, starting to shiver.

I made my way back to the station, hoping to find somewhere out of the bitter wind, but to no avail. Pacing up and down, I spotted what looked like a shed through the gathering mist, beyond the end of the platform. I jumped off the platform onto the tracks and made my way toward it, the fog thickening by the minute. It was a small wooden shed, probably for keeping tools in or maybe for housing some of the switch gear. I tried the door handle, knowing full well it would be locked. I wasn't disappointed. I put my shoulder to it in frustration and nearly fell inside as the door swung wide open. *Great security!* I thought as I stepped inside.

I quickly closed the door behind me, shutting out the icy breeze that curled the mist in through the gap. I pulled the curtains off one window and spread them out on the floor. Then I took the curtains off the second window, lay down on my impromptu bedding and pulled them over me like a blanket. Curled up tight, my knees tucked into my stomach, I cursed myself as I drifted into an uncomfortable slumber.

I woke the next morning stiff with cold, threw back the curtains (not quite in the conventional fashion), then stretched for a second before stepping outside into thick fog. I couldn't make out the platform I'd come from, but I moved toward it anyway, following the tracks. I must have made quite a picture for those standing on the platform above me on their way to work as, out of the fog, I emerged, still in my work clothes, my eyes barely open, my hair all over the place. I staggered to the end of the platform, climbed up onto it, then casually strolled in amongst the throng of commuters. *See,* I thought to myself. *It's OK. I'm one of you lot!*

Walking in the door at 7:25 AM, with just enough time to change my clothes for another day of tree planting, I found my flatmate, Simon, in the kitchen making tea.

"Hey! That's my mate! Good job, son!" he greeted me enthusiastically in his rich Zimbabwean accent.

I stood like a zombie, not quite comprehending where he was coming from. Then the penny dropped. He was convinced I'd gotten lucky, that I had spent what turned out to be the coldest night that winter wrapped in the arms of a woman.

"Mate, believe me. Nothing could be further from the truth!"

Realization

Wheeling myself slowly into the bathroom, I catch my reflection in the mirror as I turn to close the door. *God! My eyes! Look at my eyes!* The pupils have dilated from the morphine, giving me a manic, crazed look. I look like Charles Manson. *No wonder I'm freaking people out.* Seeing myself in the wheelchair like this, I realize for the first time how other people see me now, how they'll see me for the rest of my life. My head reels at the thought and I feel my heart sink as the consequences unfold before me.

This is it, isn't it? This is a life sentence. This is how I'll look when I die. This is how my kids are going to see me. How will they cope, having an old man who's a freak? How will they feel when other kids at school laugh at me and point?

I stare intently at the image before me, a towel discreetly over my lap. "What do I really look like?" I wonder. I remove the towel, then, with both hands on the armrests of the wheelchair, I raise myself up out of the seat. I stare in horror and disbelief.

Nothing could have prepared me for what I'm seeing.

"Jesus Christ!" I gasp aloud.

The shock of seeing myself like this for the first time is overwhelming, the impact so strong. I've been looking down my body at the place where my legs used to be for a few weeks now and have become relatively accustomed to the sight. But this is something else. *This is how other people see me.* I can't stop looking, fascinated that I can look like this, so utterly transformed. My legs are so much smaller now that I'm seeing them in proportion with the rest of my body. All that remains are two stumps. They just hang there under me, like two legs of ham, as I hold myself up. I can't take my eyes away. *It's no wonder people stare the way they do.*

I've been using the wheelchair for a few days now, but I still can't comprehend the role it will play in the rest of my life. At first, I saw it only as a temporary tool to get me to the shower or toilet. It felt awkward to use and I was afraid of falling out of it. My fragility scared me. Every little bump I came across sent a jolt of pain through my legs. But I've begun to accept the inevitable: *This is it, mate. You are now, officially, a cripple.*

Enter Sunshine

Finally, the day arrives when I get to leave the hospital building for the first time. With Dad pushing me, we make our way through the maze that is the hospital, through corridors that all look the same. (Correct me if I'm wrong, I'm not claiming to be an expert on hospitals, but aren't they all like this? A maze—to throw the dazed patient, already totally disorientated, into further confusion.) Along the way, Mom gives me a commentary on the different wards I've been in, where different things are and so on. Then, from the elevator on the ground floor, Dad wheels me out through the glass front doors and into sunlight. Three weeks have passed since I last saw the sun, and I wince immediately at the intensity of the glare.

"That bloody sun's bright!" I complain, with one hand covering my eyes. "I think I need some shades!"

My eyes have become used to the dim hospital lights and are now being overwhelmed by the midday sun. We make a beeline for a store in front of the hospital, into which Mom darts, quickly returning with a bottle of mineral water (I'm still constantly thirsty and hadn't thought to bring a drink) and a pair of sunglasses.

With the glare problem sorted out, I begin to appreciate the heat of the sun as it beats down on me. It feels incredible on my skin after what has seemed like an eternity of lying in bed inside the dull confines of the hospital. Crossing the road to a stretch of parkland between the Esplanade and the sea, Dad points to a concrete pad set in the middle with a path connecting it to the road.

"That's where the helicopter landed when they flew you here." I don't recognize it at all. I remember feeling like we landed on the roof of the hospital, not across the road from it.

We carry on along a concrete path through the park, Dad pushing me the whole time. It feels so strange. I can't help thinking that it must be nearly thirty years since he last pushed me like this—in a stroller. I can't possibly conceive how he must be feeling about pushing me in a wheelchair now, but I soon lose this train of thought with what happens next: Approaching another road to cross, I notice the distinct lack of a curb ramp in the path. The curb drops straight onto the road. I'm wondering what we are going to do when, without warning, the chair tips back beneath me.

"Bloody hell!" I yell out, holding on to the chair so tight that my knuckles must be white. "What are you doing?"

My cry has scared Dad just as much as his quickly executed mono has me. "Shit, sorry, mate," he apologizes. "Are you all right?"

"Yeah, I suppose," I answer, still shaking. "I might have to change my undies when we get back, but apart from that, I'm fine." This time I'm ready, as Dad tilts me back, then lowers me on the chair's back wheels over the curb. Only when the front wheels touch the ground do I begin to relax. Mom thinks the curb episodes are hilarious. Because she was standing ahead the first time, waiting for us, she could see both our faces: Dad's smiling face as he set about tackling his first wheelchair obstacle, and the look of sheer terror on mine as I felt the chair tip out from under me. It must have been quite a sight. We're still laughing about it as we arrive back in the dreary scenario of E West ward, just in time for dinner.

Progress at Last

Eventually my wounds heal well enough for the dressings to be changed in the ward; previously that's only been done in surgery. Consequently, I haven't actually seen my stumps naked yet, only the shape of them wrapped in bandages. This time, the nurse carefully unravels the dressing of my right leg as I look on with a combination of morbid fascination and something best described as revulsion. The normal procedure with an amputation is to leave flaps of skin beyond the actual amputation site, then sew these together over the stump end. But because I've had so many operations there hasn't been a lot of skin left to work with. The two flaps on each leg are stretched so tightly that, to keep them together, the fishing line (yes, *fishing* line) they've used is threaded through what looks like plastic macaroni. These act as pressure dispersers, allowing the stitching to be pulled as tight as possible without cutting through my flesh. The visual effect can only be described as looking like something out of a Frankenstein movie. *God! I'm glad Mom's not here to see this!*

She does, though, a few days later, when she pops her head around the curtain as they're changing my dressings, catching me unawares before I have a chance to warn her. I cringe as I see her looking at my legs. I feel almost embarrassed by the revulsion I'm sure she's feeling. Much to my relief, she handles it much better than I think she will.

"They're a bit of a mess, aren't they?" she remarks, biting her bottom lip in a look of concern and sympathy.

"They're not bad," I reply, breathing a sigh of relief that she hasn't recoiled from the sight. Deep down, it signifies an acceptance. The thought of my own mother being repulsed by my new form would devastate me. Thankfully, it's a thought I can put out of my mind.

Three weeks after losing my legs, I can finally see some light at the end of the tunnel. Arrangements are being made to get me admitted to a hospital down in Melbourne, and I haven't had any surgery for more than a week! Also, my appetite has returned, though I think that has something to do with the nutritionist recommending that, if I didn't start eating more protein, they would have to recommence nightly drip feeds via a nasal tube (a joy left behind upon leaving intensive care). *No thanks! I think I feel hungry again now.*

My strength is improving also. I can do a couple of chin-ups on the bar above my bed and, shuffling across on my bum, get in and out of the wheelchair. Although when it's suggested that I spend some time sitting in the chair beside my bed to prepare me for the flight to Melbourne,

I think it's a bit of a joke. *Practise sitting down! Yeah, right, what do they think I am?*

I've never actually thought about gravity much. Apart from its habit of holding me to the ground, it has remained inconspicuous—until now, after I've been lying flat on my back for three weeks. After a mere thirty minutes' sitting in the chair, I can't believe how tired I am. I can feel the weight of every organ hanging in my chest, as if I'm being pulled to the ground by my insides. I sit slumped in the chair for another five minutes before I have to climb wearily into bed to lie down. I feel like a 90-year-old man! "How long does it take to fly to Melbourne?" I ask Dad during one of these "sits."

"About four hours," he replies.

"*Great! Looks like I've got some training to do.*"

Home

Friday, May 9, 1997. Mom's birthday. What better present could she have hoped for than for all of us to be flying home? The day has finally arrived. I've been declared "fit to fly." The three of us are booked on a 9 PM flight.

For the most part, the day drags on like any other, until the mad rush begins at about 6 PM. The nurse, changing my dressings for the last time, pokes around as if she has all day, leaving us with little time to spare as we race to the taxi stand in front of the hospital to find . . . no taxi. Dad is ropeable. He storms off to find a telephone and has a cab at the curb in a few minutes.

We finally arrive at the airport, but only after enduring the driver's whining about how he always has to wait for people. *Yeah, yeah.* I think to myself. *I'd like to have a dollar for every hour I've spent waiting for taxis in my life. I'd be flying home in a Lear jet.*

Paul and Karen are waiting in front of the airport terminal when we arrive. They've been fantastic, looking after Mom and Dad all these weeks, giving them much needed space and support. I thank them both as a Qantas attendant helps me transfer into another wheelchair, an extremely narrow one without armrests, designed for moving down aircraft aisles. I feel uneasy in a chair without armrests, worried I might lose my balance and fall out. The last thing I need right now is to damage my stumps. I've spent all the time I want, and more, in the Cairns Base Hospital.

There aren't more than fifty people on board the plane, including the pilots and cabin crew. The flight began in Osaka and this is its only stop before it arrives in Melbourne. Down the aisle I'm wheeled, toward the back of the plane. Halfway down, we reach my seat; all nine of them. The seat backs are folded forward with a stretcher sitting on top. This puts me up under the overhead luggage bins, directly under the lights and personal air vents. I'm facing the back of the plane; all I can see are empty seats. All the other passengers are seated up toward the front of the plane, behind me.

Nervous thoughts fill my head as to what will happen if something goes wrong and we have to evacuate the plane. I have visions of people screaming and rushing for the exit doors as the plane bursts into flames, leaving me strapped in, unable to escape. I feel incredibly vulnerable, yet again, it's something I suspect I'm going to have to get used to.

Surely nothing can happen to me now, I reassure myself, not after everything I've been through. Could any god, or dealer of fate, be so cruel as to have me die in a plane crash now? After all this? I hope not. Sensing my anxiety, one of the flight stewards takes the time to assure me that they'll get me out if there's an emergency. And as the front wheel lifts off the ground, I close my eyes and succumb to a relative calm. What lies ahead of me, I don't know, but that has never worried me in the past. And it doesn't concern me now. I'm alive after coming so close to death that I smelt like it. And now I'm heading home!

PART III

THE
RECLAMATION

In wilderness is the preservation of Mankind.

HENRY THOREAU

The Journey Begins

I'm admitted to the Royal Talbot Rehabilitation Centre in Melbourne at about 2 AM Saturday morning, having come straight from the airport. The whole family had been there to greet us. Lisa and Michelle organized a wheelchair for me and a disabled taxi stood waiting for us outside the arrivals terminal. We traveled in a convoy, Mom and I in the taxi (me in the back in the wheelchair, which was strapped to anchors in the floor of the cab), the rest of the family in two cars behind us.

I had no idea what lay in store for me at the rehab center. Sitting in the taxi, staring anxiously out the window, I wondered what was going to happen next. Until that point it had all been about recovery. But I wanted to do more than recover. I wanted to know my limits. *Have I been reduced to needing one of these special taxi cabs every time I need to go somewhere?* So far, all I had were questions—lots of them.

We had been assured, though it would be the middle of the night, that someone would be there to admit me, but the doors are locked and the place looks deserted when we arrive. Mom buzzes an intercom, and, within a few minutes, the duty nurse appears. She opens the huge glass door and ushers us all inside. As you would expect at this hour of the morning, the place is deathly silent. I follow her down a corridor, everybody else behind me, until she stops in front of a doorway to the left and motions me inside.

"Your bed is in here," she says quietly.

"No worries, whereabouts?" I ask, poised in the doorway, my eyes still adjusting to the darkness.

"This way," she replies, and I follow her to a bed in the far corner of the room, past half a dozen others that appear occupied. "Here," she says.

I thank her, then turn back toward the door, where my family are watching with interest.

"Do you need some help to get in?" the nurse asks, throwing me completely.

"No, I don't," I reply. "I need a coffee or something first. I haven't even said goodbye to these guys yet." It's a bizarre moment. As if I'm going to just wheel over and hop into bed, without even saying goodbye!

"Ah, yes. OK," she replies, and directs us into the communal dining-lounge area. After a quick coffee (the silence of a hospital at 2:30 AM isn't the most relaxed atmosphere in which to sit and chat), we say our goodbyes and I make my way back to bed.

So begins my stay at the Royal Talbot.

THE THING that strikes me first upon waking the next morning is the feeling that I've moved into a nursing home. Of the five guys in my room, two of them look like they may not live to see the sun go down. Being a Saturday, nothing is happening, and patients are sitting around, left to their own resources. I learn that, on Monday, I'll meet with the team assigned to rehabilitate me. In the meantime, an interim doctor pays me a visit, going through my medical history before asking me the million-dollar question:

"So, what do you hope to achieve in here, Warren? What is your goal?"

I know what I want to do. I've known right from the start, but I haven't really talked about it with anyone until now.

"I want to walk again," I answer, matter-of-factly.

"Mmmmm," he replies, hand on his chin. "That's going to be very difficult you know, Warren. It will take a lot of work."

"Yes, I reckon it will." I'm taken aback by his response, not so much by his words but from the sense of pity that accompanies them.

"You see, it takes an incredible amount of effort to walk as an above-knee amputee. I've seen the results of a study that shows an above-knee amputee uses up to two hundred per cent more energy than an average person just to walk," he says, obviously warning me not to get my hopes up too high.

"Mate, I'll be happy enough just to walk out of here," is my comeback. "What happens after that, we'll have to wait and see." I don't like his attitude in trying to quash my aspirations, and his suggestion that I might not be able to walk triggers a desire to prove him wrong.

He continues, "See, your stumps are very short. You may not be able to use prostheses at all. We'll have to wait and see what the prosthetist says, whether he thinks he'll be able to help you."

Nobody has raised the issue of the length of my stumps until now; I've presumed that it will just be a matter of a lot of hard work before I will walk again. It hasn't occurred to me that it may not be possible. After he leaves, I lay back on my bed, head swimming at the notion that I may not be able to walk again. The thought leaves me depressed, a feeling that will hang over me like a black cloud until Monday morning and my meeting with the prosthetist. In the meantime I explore the hospital, getting used to moving about in the wheelchair.

Over the weekend, I meet another couple of young guys, which helps me feel a bit more at home, not so out of place. Dallas is a great guy who has been doing it pretty hard over the last few years; his body has basically given up on him after years of abuse and neglect. Mark rode his motorbike into the front of a truck, smashing one leg so badly he may yet lose it. The three of us, later joined by Lloyd, will spend a fair amount of time together over the coming months, including sneaking out for a pizza and beers every now and then.

Monday morning. The five members of my rehabilitation team gather around my bed: Jeanett Hofland, the doctor in charge of the amputee unit; John Semmens, the prosthetist; Liz Howard, my occupational therapist; Belinda Walsh, my physiotherapist; and the amputee unit's nurse (whose name now escapes me). The curtain is drawn around my bed before the nurse begins removing my dressings. I feel extremely nervous—not because of the attention to my wounds (I'm used to that by now); it's the consequences of what it will mean if John decides he can't help me that worry me. The relief that sweeps over me when he leans forward, takes a good look at my stumps, and proclaims, "Yeah, I reckon we can do something with those," is enormous.

OK then. That's all I need to hear!

I throw myself into rehab like a man possessed. I have to give myself the best possible chance of success and that means being as fit as possible. But wheeling into the amputee unit's gym, I'm startled at first by the sight of all the people with various missing limbs. Then again, I probably freak them out as well; they all have more in the leg department than I've been left with.

The first objective is to get my balance back. Losing so much weight
in the form of my legs has thrown my balance off completely. I have to
be very careful just sitting up so that I don't topple over backward without my legs to counterbalance me. We start with me sitting up on a
treatment bed and Belinda standing in front of me, throwing a tennis
ball between us. When that gets too easy, we move on to using bats,
turning the exercise into a form of aerial table tennis. From there, we
graduate to a medicine ball. Now it's getting interesting! The first time
she throws it to me, it knocks me over backward. But the workout it
gives my stomach muscles is incredible. When I catch it off to one side, I
spin around with it, carried through by the ball's momentum. But I
think I'm doing well with all this balance stuff—until she brings over the
Swiss ball and explains what she wants me to do.

Easing myself off the edge of the bed, Belinda on one side of me and
Allison (her assistant) on the other, I cautiously shift my weight onto
the pressure ball, my stomach tensing as the ball moves about. Suddenly, it rolls from under me. I'm too slow to throw my hips forward
and have to be grabbed by the girls to keep from falling. My near spill
gives me quite a start, and my stomach is still doing cartwheels as they
help me back on.

"Yeah, right! Great game this is!" I laugh nervously, sure that they've
set me an impossible task.

"You'll be all right." Belinda assures me, having a bit of a giggle herself. "That was good. I think you'll do really well on this."

Around the same time, I begin using what is commonly known as a
"wobble board." A plywood disc (about 400 millimeters/16 inches in diameter) with a halved plastic ball attached to one side, the wobble board
becomes my favorite toy. Placed on the floor, ball side down, it presents
an extremely unstable seat. Just being able to sit on it is an achievement
in itself. But in the beginning, I can't stay on it for more than a few seconds before falling off. It, too, gives my stomach muscles an incredible
workout, and that alone is incentive enough for me to get on it at every
opportunity. Resigned to the fact that, because I'm spending so much
time sitting down, the spare tire around my waist is now part of the

furniture, the wobble board provides a glimmer of hope that maybe, just maybe . . .

The only thing holding me back now is the wound at the back of my left stump that still hasn't healed. It began as a graze, possibly from the initial impact when I slammed into the riverbed under the weight of the rock. In Cairns it turned into a bed sore and became infected. But until it heals to a point that the doctors are happy with, I won't be able to begin prosthetic training. I vent my frustration through exercise, obsessed with getting fit.

A back injury, incurred a year or so ago, particularly concerns me. If there is one thing that might stop me from walking again, this is it. I incorporate some basic yoga into my routine with the specific aim of strengthening my back. It must be quite a sight for visitors to the amputee gym to be greeted with the vision of a legless man in a shoulder stand at the back of the room. Each afternoon, I also go through a set program using free weights in the center's main gym, run by Wayne Dite. I think Wayne gets a kick out of having someone using his domain the way I do. My attitude is markedly different from those of his average clients, many of whom are here under duress, being pushed along reluctantly. But I'm on a mission! I want to get myself into the best possible shape so that when the time comes to walk again, my body will be ready. Only forces outside my control will stop me. I've always had to work extremely hard to stay fit. Now, unable to walk, I find it even harder; no matter how much exercise I do, I always feel like I need more.

"I really need to be swimming," I keep saying to anyone who will listen, convinced I need to be working on my aerobic fitness. But I can't start swimming until my wound has healed; it's too risky for me to swim in the hydrotherapy pool with an open wound (albeit, dressed), for my health and others'. I'm told that, when I'm ready to use the pool, I'll have to be lowered into the water on a hoist, for safety reasons.

"Sorry, but you can forget that," I reply. I'm not about to suffer the indignity of being lowered into the pool like a rescued whale—not after reading how Douglas Bader, the famous World War II fighter pilot, went about his first swim after he lost both legs in an aircraft accident.

After pulling himself up the ladder of the diving tower, he shuffled to the end of the board, went into a handstand, then dove off.

"No, I'll be going in off the side, at the very least. That, or I'll go and swim somewhere else."

Looking Forward

Two or three weeks after my admittance, it's suggested that I am well enough to go home to Mom and Dad's on the weekends. Jeanette Holland, my doctor, recalls that my sister Michelle is a nurse and asks if she could change my dressings over the weekends. Michelle enthusiastically agrees, and, with that, arrangements to get me home—albeit only for the weekends—begin. Dad fixes a couple of handrails in the bathroom, and we borrow a ramp that clears three steps at the back door.

It feel so good coming up the driveway to our house, like another piece of my life has fallen back into place. Sitting at the kitchen table with Mom and Dad is such a simple act, yet it symbolizes my return to the world in a grand way. I start to feel like a normal person again. Being in a hospital tends to strip away your character, your identity; you start to mould to the form of "patient." I think it's got something to do with being surrounded by sick people. Unless you really fight it, the negative, somber atmosphere can drag you down with it.

I decided relatively early in my rehab that I needed to be able to get in and out of my wheelchair from the floor. I'm certain to fall out of it at some point. It's only a matter of time. But the thought of being stranded somewhere, or falling out in public and having people help me back in, terrifies me. It's not the falling out part; that doesn't worry me so much, but I have always had a problem with asking people to do things for me. I hate relying on others.

Helen, my new physiotherapist, helps me get started. She explains that getting from the floor onto something as high as the wheelchair is quite an undertaking, and that to start off we need to tackle smaller heights first, then gradually work up to the chair. I begin with a 13-centimeter (5-inch) step, sitting with my back to it, both hands reaching behind me, palms on top of the step. Pulling in through my stomach muscles and pushing with my triceps, I lift my backside up and swing back onto the step. *This isn't too difficult.* We then increase the height, and as we do so I realize that this just doesn't seem to be the right way to go about it. *There has to be a better way . . .*

One night, sitting on the living room floor at Mom and Dad's, an idea comes to me. Sitting in front of the wheelchair, my left side toward it, I keep my left hand on the front of the chair but put my right hand on the floor. Leaning forward, moving my weight over my right hand, I then lift into the air, steadying myself with my left hand. I hold my position there for a second, then swing my body up and across, catching the edge of the seat under my bum.

Yes! That's it! I've got it!

The feeling is electric. I sense the implications immediately. I'm no longer "confined" to the wheelchair. I can get in and out when I please. I can leave it behind if it gets in the way. It's my first taste of freedom in a long time, and it feels exquisite.

WHEN SOMEONE suggests that I might see the hospital's psychologist, I'm a little put out.

"Why, do you think I'm going to lose the plot or something?" is my initial response.

"No. It's a standard requirement in everyone's rehabilitation, just to make sure you're coping with things mentally as well as physically," is the explanation.

"OK, then." *This should be interesting.*

Expecting some middle-aged, tweed-jacketed, pipe-smoking eccentric, I'm pleasantly surprised to meet Daphne Smith, my psychologist. Still, at our first meeting, though we just chat casually, telling stories about what we've done and where we've been, I feel very much on guard. I figure a psychologist's job is to take a person apart piece by piece, then put them back together again. It's a bit dramatic I know, but that's how I feel.

At my next appointment, I begin to relax, and eventually I start to look forward to our meetings. They gave me the chance to talk to somebody, not in a "purging my soul" sense, but in the sense of having a sounding board—someone who seems interested in what I've done, how I'm coping now, what I want to do, and so on. (Unfortunately, Daphne's contract with the center comes to an end a few weeks later— budgets are tight within the health care system and, apparently, the patients' mental state isn't that important. Still, I keep in touch with Daphne outside of the hospital, gaining strength from her encouragement and support.)

—— BACK ATTACK ——

The time I spent campaigning against the building of the Link Road in the Tarkine opened my eyes to what I really wanted to do with my life. I decided then and there that the only way we could get people to value the wilderness was to show it to them—not on TV, but by taking them into it. I wanted to give people a taste of what I felt every time I walked out into the bush, my sense of rejuvenation at being immersed in nature. But in December 1995, after an epic struggle resulting in more than one hundred arrests, the battle for the Donaldson River came to an end. We had lost, and though we realized there were still avenues to explore in ensuring protection of the area (many continue to campaign for the Tarkine to be granted World Heritage Area status, for which it has since been recommended), for many of us the bridging of the river symbolized the end of the campaign. I became thoroughly disillusioned with everything. What had we achieved? Anything?

It took me a while to appreciate that we had accomplished a great deal. There wasn't a single person left in Tasmania who now hadn't heard of the Tarkine, and that wouldn't have happened if we had stood quietly by. What we needed to do in the coming years was *show* it to them. And who was in a better position to do that than us, the Tarkine Tigers, who had fought so hard to save it? We even had our own trails that no one else knew about. But first, it was time to rest, time to recoup some energy after our enormous struggle.

I spent a couple of weeks traveling around the state, sleeping under the stars at Sisters Beach on the north coast, exploring new forests, swimming in wild rivers. Jarrah, whom I'd first met on the Roger trip, told me one night about a course he was thinking of taking, an adventure tour guide program that would give him the qualifications he needed to work as an outdoor guide. It sounded like an excellent idea. If we were going to set ourselves up as a company running trips through the Tarkine, it made sense to have some recognized qualifications. One evening, as we sat around the table in a hut high on Mount Dundas in the state's west, Jarrah casually mentioned that applications for the course closed the next day, at midday.

"Tomorrow?" I asked.

"Yeah, I think it's tomorrow," he replied.

"Shit. We'd better go into town tomorrow and find out."

First thing in the morning, three of us packed and hiked back down the mountain: Jarrah, myself, and Andrew Devine. We drove into the nearest town, Zeehan (an old mining town), where we had no trouble finding the post office (it's a small town), and used the phone to ring the number Jarrah had been given. A guy called Brian Hall was running the course. He said we needed to complete an application form, which was no problem—he could fax one to us. *Excellent!* As soon as it came through, we found a place to have breakfast and filled in our applications over toast and coffee. We then faxed the forms back to Brian, then rang him to make sure he had received them. In the afternoon, we drove the two hours to Devonport to get ready for our interviews the following day.

The next morning, at my interview, I hit it off well with Brian right from the start. Brian had that unique mix of professionalism and fun. He was always smiling. I felt I stood a good chance of getting into the course; and sure enough, Jarrah and I started a week later, with Andrew missing out because of his age (too young). Almost immediately, it was clear that this was exactly what I was meant to do—that this was what I'd been heading toward for some time.

The next month was spent learning the commercial side of adventure travel. We then spent a couple of days rafting on the Upper Mersey River, followed by some time around Cradle Mountain, including climbing to its summit one glorious afternoon. After that, we had a break of four weeks before the next training block began, a good opportunity to catch up with family and friends back in Melbourne and Brisbane. I had been away for a year. But several weeks later, when I rang Brian from Melbourne one afternoon to confirm the starting date of the second training block, he told me the bad news. We'd just had a federal election and, with the change in government, all funding for Skillshare courses had been temporarily frozen. That included ours.

"Give me a ring in another few weeks, Waz. Something may have happened by then," he advised, disappointment in his voice. So I did, but by then the news was even worse. The course funding had been frozen indefinitely—it looked likely that it would be scrapped altogether.

After my initial disappointment, I decided that I would go back to Tassie and do the courses independently. But it was going to cost me a fair bit of money, which I didn't have, and with winter coming on I couldn't expect to rely on painting work. I rang Athos Venturi, a landscaping contractor I'd worked for a few years before in Melbourne.

"Yeah, mate. I reckon I might have some work for you," he said.

"Excellent! When can I start?"

I worked for Athos for the next few months, at one stage using a Bobcat (a small, skid-steer earth mover) to shift topsoil on a building site. I must have had a stupid grin on my face whenever I drove that Bobcat. Only months before, in the Tarkine, I'd been arrested after having to be cut from beneath a bulldozer with an angle grinder. I found it quite bizarre now to be using the tools of the "enemy." The money was beginning to build up; it wouldn't be long before I could head back down to Tassie and get back on track.

It was around this time that my back began to get sore and stiff in the winter cold. I figured it meant I was just getting too old for construction work, too weak. But then one morning I had trouble even reaching down to pull my boots on, as the pain stabbed into my back. Ambling into work, I said to Ath's partner, Tony:

"Mate, I hope you haven't got much planned for today, because I'm not going to be worth two cents." I told him what the problem was and made sure he gave me all the easy jobs to do for the day. But it wasn't enough. I woke the next day in agony. It was difficult to even get out of bed. I couldn't reach my feet at all. Something was badly wrong: the pain was unlike anything I'd felt before, like something inside me was physically restricting my movement. I made an appointment with a local doctor, who sent me off for X-rays. Back at the doctor's for the results, I sat and listened as he brought my world undone with his news. I had damaged one of the discs in my back, he explained. But he didn't think my injury was that bad—as long as I didn't lift anything heavy, I'd be fine. I sat there astounded.

"Not that bad? Were you listening when I told you what I do for a living," I responded angrily.

"People have much worse injuries," he replied.

"I'm sure they do. But they're probably sitting at home right now on the couch, watching TV!"

I left the clinic absolutely shattered, unable to think of anything apart from what I wouldn't be able to do. *I'll never be able to carry a backpack again. How am I going to travel if I can't pick up any kind of work?* My whole lifestyle revolved around freedom, being able to come and go as I pleased, picking up work whenever I needed it. I couldn't imagine what I'd do with that freedom taken from me. *That's it, mate. You're finished!*

Over the following weeks, I sank into a downward spiral of depression at the uncertainty that lay ahead. I had never had to face anything like this before. Sure, I'd been injured—but always temporarily. I'd never had to face the prospect of not being able to do something ever again. Facing that reality terrified me. At Mom's suggestion, I saw a physiotherapist. He made the situation very clear for me, but gave me some desperately needed hope. He mentioned a football player who lived with much the same injury as mine.

"He never gets to play the whole season, and he puts in a lot of work to play the games he does. But he plays."

That was all I needed to hear. *If someone with a damaged disc can run around a football field like those maniacs do, I can carry a pack!* The therapist then gave me a series of stretches and exercises to do and suggested I swim as often as possible. I immediately swung into action, eager to get my life back. Within a month I began to see results as I religiously went through the exercises that would strengthen the muscles around the injury in my lower back. (Although the injured disc could literally take years to heal, by strengthening the muscles around it I could take the pressure off the damaged area.) By the time the second month rolled around, I felt ready for the true test, and spent a weekend hiking with a light pack at Wilson's Promontory, a national park east of Melbourne. The simple act of carrying that pack gave an enormous boost to my confidence. So much so, that I decided that rather than continue my re-cuperation in the depths of another depressing, rainy Melbourne win-ter, I would head north to Queensland and get well in the sunshine. I figured that within six months I could get myself strong enough to carry a full pack again, during which time I would begin my river guide certification in Tully (a small town in North Queensland that, with an average rainfall of more than 1,000 millimeters (40 inches) each year, is a major whitewater rafting center). I would then make my way back to Tassie in time for the summer guiding season. It seemed like such a good plan. Destiny however, had other ideas . . .

LOOKING BACK now, I'm sure that going through that experience with my back is helping me cope with losing my legs. When I first injured my back, I thought my life as I knew it was over. And in a way, it was. Al-though I wasn't as restricted as I initially thought, the injury would limit what I would be able to do—forever. So I've already gone through some of the pain that I'm feeling now, the mental anguish of having some-thing taken away from me—albeit a fraction of what was still to come. But I've been through it once already, nevertheless, and I'm sure that it softened the blow.

Back on the Road

The next step in regaining my freedom is driving again. My occupa-tional therapist has made arrangements for a lesson with a driving school that has cars fitted with hand-controlled gas and brake pedals.

Sliding out of my chair and in behind the wheel feels surreal. I put my seat belt on, and, as I buckle up, I look down at the space between the pedals on the floor and my thighs. It's one of those moments when every-thing comes back to me: the stark reality of *yes, you've got no legs*. I try to picture my legs reaching down to the pedals but can't. It sounds insane, but the distance seems too great, I can't imagine my legs ever having been long enough to reach the pedals. By this stage, I'm having trouble picturing how far out from the end of my stumps my knees used to be.

Pulling out into the stream of traffic, I'm amazed at how confident I feel. It really isn't as difficult as I'd imagined. I've been having visions of an absolutely hopeless scenario—of going for the brake pedal with a foot that isn't there.

I drive with the instructor for forty-five minutes around the northern suburbs of Melbourne before returning to the Talbot.

"Well, how did I do?" I ask.

"No problems at all," he replies, and that's it. I've passed, and reclaimed another piece of my life.

Meanwhile, my car is on the back of a truck, being shipped down from Northern Queensland. (Rob Baines, the painting contractor I was working for at the time of the accident, brought it back from Cardwell and arranged for it to be transported to Melbourne.) As soon as it arrives, I arrange for it to be fitted with the same hand controls as I used with the driving instructor. Driving my own car again for the first time feels incredible. Driving across town to visit Lisa and Per one Friday night, I almost feel *normal* again. As I sit at the traffic lights, I think of how I must look to other drivers, how average I must appear. I feel in a way that I'm deceiving them, going under false pretences. I dread more than anything the prospect of an accident, that I'll be looked upon as someone who "shouldn't have been driving anyway." But in a mischievous way, I'm looking forward to picking up my first hitchhiker.

Standing Tall

On June 24, just ten weeks after losing my legs, I stand in prosthetic legs for the first time. John stands before me, within the parallel bars, while Allison stands behind. Everyone in the room has stopped what they were doing and is watching, waiting. Balanced on the front edge of my wheelchair seat, a hand on each of the bars in front of me, I ease my backside forward and transfer my weight to what is left of my hamstring muscles. I push down through my stumps, riding the articulated linkages that are my new legs up until my body is directly above my new feet. The titanium knees snap into place beneath me.

"How does that feel?" John asks, eyes level with mine for the first time.

Relaxing my arms slightly, I let my stumps take a little more weight, completely absorbed by the incredible feeling of standing again. It is some moments before I manage to answer.

"Pretty good," I reply, always the champion of the understatement, an uncontrollable grin the only indication of the excitement that's boiling up within me. I feel an overwhelming sense of pride that they are seeing the real me at last. That, for this moment, they can see past the image of the cripple and catch a glimpse of me as the "real person": the way I once was, the way I still feel inside. I feel like I'm showing them my most prized possession, and their smiles of encouragement have me battling to control my emotions.

As I stand savoring all of these incredible feelings, John gets to work with his allen key, adjusting the alignment of my new knees. (John is quite the artist. At one point, he tells me he'd like to make me a pair of "Terminator" legs—just like the ones Arnie sports in the movie.) Around my waist, I'm wearing a plastic brace, complete with "six-pack" abs. Fixed to my laminate sockets with hinged metal braces, it acts like a splint, supporting my torso in case my hips are not strong enough to do so.

Standing back in front of me again, John says, "There you go, try that. Let's see if you can take a few steps." I look up in surprise, my excitement tainted with uncertainty.

"Can I?" I ask, still getting used to the idea that I'm actually standing. I haven't dared let my mind wander any further forward—the enormity of standing hasn't fully sunk in yet.

"I don't see why not," he answers. "We're both here to catch you." Allison moves my wheelchair so she can get in behind me.

"I've got your knees adjusted for maximum safety, so you'll probably have trouble "breaking" them," John begins, explaining how each knee is meant to be snapped open as I kick a leg forward, then, after I swing it through underneath me, it will snap closed with the help of a return spring, allowing me to safely transfer my weight onto it. "For now, just try and walk with straight legs."

"Cowboy style?" I suggest, smiling.

"Yeah, something like that," he laughs.

Taking more weight through my arms again, I lift my right hip, tilting my pelvis until one paint-spattered sand shoe leaves the floor. (These old work shoes get a few laughs, but I'm not ready to spend money on new shoes just yet.) The prosthesis feels quite heavy as I swing it forward with the little leverage my stump provides and, twisting my hips, place the foot down just in front of the left. Lifting myself with the bars, I then step back slightly to get my balance. As I draw in a deep breath, Neil Armstrong's famous words from 1969 echo through my mind: "One small step for a man . . ."

I've taken my first step.

Another Operation

I'm increasingly disillusioned with the progress of my left stump. Although the wound at the back of my thigh isn't stopping me from walking, it doesn't seem to be healing at all. In fact, I'm trying to avoid focusing on it because it actually seems to be getting worse. It's healing from the edges in, rather than from the bottom up. Although the surface hole is barely big enough to fit a matchstick into, it's still about 1.5 centimeters (.6 inch) deep, and I'm afraid that it's getting deeper. I'm worried that it's taking so long to heal, but I'm being constantly reassured that it's OK.

The prospect of another operation, of losing more of my leg, chills me. I can't think about it without sinking into a pit of depression. *Will this ever be over?* I try to convince myself that there isn't a problem; that the doctors know what they're doing, that worrying about it will only make things worse. I concentrate on the theory that, if I dwell on the negative aspects of something for too long, I *could* actually be making it worse— manifesting something that isn't there to begin with. (Several weeks from now, I'll wish I had followed my gut feeling, but *hindsight* is just that.)

When it finally becomes obvious that the stump isn't healing, arrangements are made for me to have a Sinu-gram—a test in which the wound cavity is filled with Contrast, a liquid that shows up on X-rays. The test will determine whether the wound is "tracking" (when the infection spreads deeper into the tissue, complicated by healing at the surface). As I lay on the X-ray bench, watching the image of my leg on the monitor while the Contrast is injected, my heart sinks at the sight of a white stain spreading slowly as it fills the cavity.

"Jesus!" I spit out. "I knew it!" I'm so angry—with myself mainly, for not acting on my gut instinct; but also at the way in which this has been allowed to get so far because the health system operates on a wait-and-see basis rather than a preventive one. The main fissure is now within a few millimeters (.08 inch) of my femur. If it had reached it, the infection could have entered the bone and I would probably have lost the majority of what remains of my left leg. It's clear to me now that, whilst the medical staff are here to help, it's me who has to be in the driver's seat. I need to take charge rather than have blind faith in others.

Ten days later, on the morning of Friday, July 25, I go into the Austin Hospital for day surgery, which leaves me with a hole underneath my left leg that is 5 by 10 centimeters (2 by 4 inches) in diameter and 7.5 centimeters (3 inches) deep. Dad and Michelle arrive to pick me up, and Michelle, who has been changing my dressings on the weekends, is briefed on my dressing requirements for the new wound. Feeling no pain as I leave, I toss the packet of Panadol the nurse has given me onto the dashboard of the car. But as the anesthetic from the surgery begins to wear off that evening, a dull, throbbing ache develops that's so intense I have trouble sleeping. By morning, it has reached the point where even the strongest painkillers have no effect.

Michelle arrives midmorning to change the dressing. Unwrapping the bandages, she gasps aloud at the size of the wound. While I was under the anaesthetic, it was packed so tightly with saline-soaked gauze that she now has trouble getting it out. I have trouble staying conscious. Even after everything I've been through, the pain as Michelle pulls those dressings out is unbearable. It's like she's pulling the very bone out of my stump. Head thrown back, I rock in agony as she removes each piece of gauze, each one deeper and tighter than the last. Grimacing, she shares my distress as she pulls, distraught at having to cause me such grief. We both know all too well that the packing has to come out, and I know by the expression on her face that what lies underneath doesn't look good. She has seen some serious stuff in her time, but she can't believe the size of the hole they've left in me. Neither can I, when I use a mirror to look at it. It's so deep that I need a flashlight to see into its depths. The hole is big enough to accommodate a baby's fist. My stomach churns at the sight, and I can't help but wonder how long it's going to take to heal. I also can't believe I've been given no more than a packet of Panadol to control the pain, and Michelle calls the hospital to arrange something stronger.

For eight weeks, the wound requires dressing every day, sometimes twice a day. It will be three months before I can wear prosthetics again, or swim, so I spend all of my time at the gym. I'm determined not to let this setback slow me down any more than necessary. I take the opportunity to spend a week with friends (who have medical backgrounds and can change my dressings) in Tassie, while recuperating. The trip empowers me tremendously, reinforcing my independence as I drive around the state alone. I'm back on the road, back in control, and it feels awesome.

The Helicopter Returns

While waiting for the troublesome wound to heal, it seems like a good idea to learn how to use my wheelchair properly. So after each afternoon's workout in the gym, Wayne teaches me the skills I'll need to survive in the wheelchair-unfriendly world outside the Talbot's walls. First, he teaches me how to do a "mono" (balancing on the rear wheels only— either moving or sitting still), standing for what seems like hours behind my chair to catch me each time I overbalance. Next, I learn how to get up and down curbs and gutters, practising first on wooden platforms inside the gym. Meanwhile, I keep Wayne amused with my weekly tales of spills taken over the weekend, like the time I took a swan dive into the local video store. My brother, Brett, was taken completely by surprise as I showed him how I could get up steps. I pushed down so hard on the push-rims that my bum came up out of the seat beneath me, sending me sliding down the front of the chair, chest first onto the store's doorstep. We were both laughing about it when we got back home.

As my mobility increases, I spend more and more time away from the hospital. During the week, I often meet friends for dinner, usually at my newfound second home, the Vegie Bar, on Fitzroy's Brunswick Street. Leaving the restaurant after dinner with Daphne one night, I stop as I hear a sound in the distance, then sit frozen as the memories flood back, the steady beat of the helicopter's rotors moving closer. I think about how much I wanted to hear that sound the whole time I was trapped, the feeling of disbelief when the sound eventually came, as I held my breath, not daring to believe it was heading my way. And I think of how I felt when I finally saw it—a black, humming speck in the distance, flying toward me. Tears threaten to squeeze from my eyes as I scan the night sky, anxious to see the helicopter.

"Are you OK?" Daphne asks.

"Yeah," I reply, with a lump in my throat. "This is the first time I've seen a helicopter since Hinchinbrook." I'm still gazing skyward, not wanting her to see the tears welling in my eyes.

"How does it feel?" she asks.

"Like I'll always remember that sound as the turning point in my life," I say quietly, my voice trembling. "Until I heard that helicopter, I'd all but given up. I'd prepared myself to die. Hearing that helicopter meant that I still had a chance, when I'd given up all hope."

A single tear traces its way down my cheek as the drone of the rotors moves off into the night.

Off the Beaten Track

Up until now, the whole process of rehabilitation has been about readjusting the way I do things on a very basic level: regaining my balance; and learning how to use a wheelchair, how to walk again, and how to use my "new" body to carry out everyday tasks. This has all been fine and dandy, but one question has burnt in the back of my mind above all others: will I ever be able to get out into the outdoors again?

Until now, I've thought that that part of my life was gone forever. And in a way, I've accepted it, figuring that my legs served me well. They took me to places most people have never been, gave me experiences most people have never had. And for that I feel grateful and console myself with positive memories. But as my strength and mobility increase, I find myself pondering more and more what might be possible. I wonder where I could go, how far off the path I could get.

The time eventually arrives when I just have to get out of the city again. I need a taste of nature, and I ring Per to see what his plans are for the next few days.

"I need to get away before I go mad," is his response.

Neither of us really know where we want to go, so we head north (if in doubt, always head north). We decide on Wyperfeld National Park in the state's northwest. I've never been there before. Per has, but only as a child on a family camping trip, and he doesn't remember much about it. We arrive after dark, and Per sets off in search of firewood while I start some water boiling on the Trangia. He's having trouble finding wood, the sparsely treed campsite having been picked clean. I watch the beacon of his flashlight scour the whole area in a huge arc. To give him a hand, I sit my flashlight in the netting basket under my chair and head for the tree line. I don't realize what I'm doing until I've placed the first piece of firewood under the chair next to the flashlight. I smile to myself, the words of Stuart Tripp (a great guy I met at the Talbot) echoing through my mind: "Mate, you are doing this too easy. You can do anything. You know that, don't you?" Stuart lost a leg in a car accident a few years before. But by the smile constantly on his face, you'd think he'd found one!

Per and I don't bother to put up a tent; without a cloud in the sky, it would be a sacrilege to sleep in one. Instead, we lie on our backs, sleeping bags half open in the warm night, gazing up at the night sky. The stars glitter like scattered jewels—so much brighter now that we're away from the lights of the city. It's hard to imagine these are the same stars I lay under only six months earlier on Hinchinbrook. The contrast in circumstances is unfathomable. I feel relaxed, at ease with my exposure to the open air, reveling in my freedom—away from the confines of an enclosing structure. I've found sanctuary in the face of vulnerability. *Why is it that we live our lives within sterile structures? Why have we set out to tame the world, expanding our enclosure?* In doing so, we're losing our natural world—the world, I believe, that holds the key to our very existence. Laying myself open to the real world, I feel at peace with it, as I drift off on a journey through the dreamscape, the campfire embers glowing softly beside me.

After a quick breakfast and the mandatory cups of coffee, we decide to "walk" a circuit that will take us about 10 kilometers (6 miles) through mallee heathland. The trail leads through an old riverbed that has become a flood plain. Now, with the salinity resulting from land clearing and the irrigation drawing water from the river, it's little more than a sandpit, and pushing along this trail is gut-busting work. The sweat pours from me as I press forward, getting constantly bogged down in deep sand. Stopping to rest frequently, I take in the dry, sparse surroundings. The mallee scrub is so different from anything I've spent time in before—mostly dry grassland with a thin covering of eucalypt. Wallabies and kangaroos graze in the distance, bouncing away upon sighting us.

On and on I push, enjoying the workout and savoring the freedom. Finally, upon reaching the gravel road, I smile to myself, knowing I've just covered 5 kilometers (3 miles) of difficult terrain. The boundaries in my mind begin to shift: I know now that I can't be confined to the concrete footpath. *If I can do this already, who knows what is possible?*

When we reach the car, I feel the satisfying exhaustion that you only get after a hard workout. And as we leave the park just on dusk, my mind wanders through the possibilities that lay before me. *I could make it down to Sealers Cove in Wilson's Promontory* (a national park east of Melbourne), I think, my mind tracing back, trying to recall the most difficult sections of the walk. I could also do some of the walks around O'Briens Crossing (a bush camp west of Melbourne, which Mom and Dad had taken us kids to since I was five or six years old). Yet I know

I'm looking for something bigger and better; something that will really push me; something that might even be considered ambitious.

I wonder if I could get up Cradle Mountain. Now that would be something! Cradle Mountain rises above the central plateau in Tasmania's World Heritage area. I've climbed it twice before. At 1,545 meters (5,068 feet), it is something that could challenge me completely yet still be achievable. *I wonder . . . could I really do it?*

The following day finds us west of Melbourne in The Grampians National Park. It is turning into another hot day, and we need a place to swim. Eventually, we find a shaded picnic area and head out along a trail cut into the hillside, the river running below. I have to jump out of the chair often, whenever the trail is too steep or the obstacles too big to get over. We reach the river at a point where it opens out into a small rock pool, and I hop out of the chair and leave it behind to climb over one boulder at a time, slowly making my way toward the water, careful not to knock my stumps on the rocks. I haven't been in the water since the accident, apart from the bathtub, due to the wound in my stump. But it's as good as healed now, and it seems fitting that my first swim should be in a place like this. I sit on the edge for a few minutes to take in my surroundings, peel off my clothes and stay at the water's edge for another moment, then lower myself in to the cold pool.

My skin tries to crawl back up my body, retreating from the water's icy touch. *Man, it's cold!* I slide further in, down moss covered rocks until the water rises to chest level. Taking a deep breath, I then lean forward and push my head under, the water racing down my back as I arch to bring my head back up.

"Shit!" I gasp heavily. "That's bloody cold!"

Per laughs from the opposite bank. He can't resist the temptation, though, and is soon in the river with me. Like a pair of lizards, we bask in the midday sun. We must be quite a sight: two guys lying naked across the rocks, one of them with no legs. It feels so good to be alive, soaking up the warmth of the sun, the trickle of the stream alongside as the birds chatter away in the trees above us, going about their daily routine despite our intrusion. I listen as the wind sweeps gently through the trees and I know. I know now that I haven't lost everything. A huge hurdle has been put in my way, along with what sometimes seem like insurmountable obstacles. But I can get over them or around them. It will take just one step at a time; I'll break everything down into small, manageable steps. It will be as simple and as difficult as that. I will need to be patient and I will need support from people prepared to adjust to my decreased mobility. I lie there smiling as another barrier fades into oblivion, the possibilities it has prevented me from realizing now spread out before me.

I'm going to climb Cradle Mountain. I can do it, I know I can.

My Mission

I return to Melbourne with a new lease on life, a purpose, a mission. Catching up with Daphne over dinner, I let it slip casually into the conversation.

"I'm going to climb Cradle Mountain, Daph."

"Cradle Mountain in Tasmania?" she replies hesitantly, not quite knowing whether to be concerned or excited.

"That's the one," I reply matter-of-factly.

"Isn't that, like, a mountain?" she asks, probably running through a list in her mind of the first signs of insanity.

"It is. But I reckon I can do it. I've thought about it and I know I can do it."

"When?" she asks, the hesitation in her face slowly replaced with excitement.

"January or February next year," I reply (it's now October 1997, six months after the accident), "while there's a good chance of fine weather."

That's it. Now that I've told someone, I have to do it. I start telling anyone else who asks what my plans are. I'm sure some people don't believe me, but that's OK. It only makes me more determined to pull it off.

I'm going to need some new equipment. A lot of my gear was lost or damaged on Hinchinbrook. I begin writing letters to outdoor retailers in Melbourne, and find a sponsor in Bogong Equipment. They have the range of gear I need and, after meeting with Simon Head, the owner, I leave with all the equipment I require. Mont, a company based in Canberra, supplies me with a shortened sleeping bag, undoubtedly the shortest they've ever made. (Although they will later alter it to make it even shorter!)

I begin a training program based around bar dips and chin-ups, increasing the repetitions as I grow stronger. Before long, I'm doing three sets of twenty bar dips and three sets of fifteen chin-ups, twice a day. But I need more. I'm not happy with my aerobic fitness or the spare tire I haven't been able to remove from around my waist. Although I have become so good on the wobble board that I can play "wobble ball," the tire has remained. (Wobble ball is a game Allison devised when she decided the wobble board was too easy for me. It's basically a modified game of tennis, played sitting down on a wobble board.)

There's only one way I can see myself getting in shape aerobically for the climb, so I take Brett with me to the local indoor swimming pool one afternoon. I have no idea what's going to happen. The swim I had in the river with Per was in only half a meter (less than 2 feet) of water, so I still have no idea how my body will float in the water. I think about the first time I sat in a bath after the accident, how I was dealt the rather humbling blow of being knocked over by the ripple I created when I sat down as "the wave" returned from the end of the bath.

I sit on the edge of the pool, with Brett standing by—no doubt wondering how he'll know whether or not he's needed—to pull me out. Pushing myself off the edge, I dive in sideways and swim straight to the bottom. My bum is trying to rise to the surface, so I swim strongly to stay down. Twisting my body around, I then make for the surface. Brett is standing eagerly at the side. "How is it?" he asks.

"All right, I think," I reply, finding it more difficult to tread water than it had been to swim under it. As I speak, my lower body slides out from under me, rising to the surface behind me. In the process, my face is pushed down into the water, which, needless to say, gives me a bit of a surprise. Rolling over, I manage to get myself upright again.

"Well, that answers that question," I call out to Brett, who is still wondering whether I need rescuing or not.

"What question's that?" he asks.

"Whether my legs used to float or not," I reply.

I feel like I'm trying to balance on a balloon under water, struggling to keep my weight over it to stop it from tipping me as it tries to surface. My legs had acted as a kind of ballast in the water; without any, I constantly have to keep my weight over my lower body.

I begin swimming seriously in the hydrotherapy pool at the Talbot. But because it's so small, I can't do proper laps. I'm unable to "kick" off the wall, so I come to a standstill at the end of each lap and completely lose all momentum. Swimming laps in a 50-meter (164-foot) pool is difficult enough for this reason; in the 10 meters (33 feet) available at the Royal Talbot, it's out of the question. My solution is to attach a line to a railing at the end of the pool, then tie the other end to a buoyancy belt around my waist. It feels pretty strange thrashing away in one spot while the other patients walk or wade up and down the pool, but I can feel it doing me good. Before long I can swim for half an hour each session at a steady pace without stopping. I begin to feel a lot fitter and start swimming regularly with Deirdre McEwan, a friend I first met at the train station in Munich, Germany. We swim as often as we can under the summer sun in the 50-meter outdoor pool in nearby Fitzroy. This gives me great satisfaction: once out of my chair and in the pool, I can hold my own with the other swimmers. In the water, I feel far from disabled.

Walk This Way

The wound on the back of my stump finally healed, it's time to recommence prosthetic training. Before, I was restricted to walking within the parallel bars, but it's time to move outside them. Standing at the end of the bars one afternoon, I take hold of the walking frame in front of me and step forward. Helen Connor and Mark McDonald, my new physios, stand to either side of me, encouraging me as I step forward slowly and make my way across the room. When I reach a treatment bed on the other side, I turn around and sit down carefully.

Sitting down and standing up are still the two most difficult aspects of walking for me. My new knees give me support only when they are extended and locked into place; they need to be "broken" for me to sit. And I need to break them carefully because, once broken, they offer no support at all. If I don't take all my weight through my arms, I'm sent straight back down into my chair much harder than I'd prefer, or straight to the ground.

Twice a day, in between rigorous training and stretching sessions, I practise walking. Some days, I can't get my prostheses to fit properly, so I take them off after walking only a few steps—the pain being unbearable. My stumps change shape constantly, despite the elastic "socks" called "shrinkers" that I wear. These are used to keep the stumps a uniform volume but they aren't doing a very good job in my case. As a result, sometimes I just can't get fully into my sockets, which makes walking impossible.

With practice, I progress to using walking-sticks, and walk up and down the corridor outside the gym. The most important milestone for me, though, is to walk around the perimeter of the building. Up the steep hill outside the gym I struggle, one step at a time, amazed at how much effort it takes to get to the top. Walking around to the front of the building, I step through the main entrance and up to reception. The girls behind the desk have never seen me out of a wheelchair and they smile in admiration. It feels so good to stand at the counter, looking over the desk at them instead of up at them. After a quick chat, I continue on down the corridor to the elevator, take it down to the second floor, then walk back to the amputee gym. I slump into my chair, exhausted. Then I begin the arduous task of taking my legs off, quickly removing the uncomfortable neoprene suspension belt from around my waist. *I've done it. I've walked around the block!* My stumps are stiff and sore and my hips ache, but it hardly matters. I know now I'm capable of walking out the front door of the hospital, and that's all that matters. I've done what I set out to do.

Still, I reach an unconscious decision after the walk: my real goal is getting to the top of the mountain, and that won't involve my prostheses. I figure I can come back to them later. And from this moment, I walk in my legs every day until I leave hospital, but concentrate mainly on my training for Cradle.

On December 19, 1997, eight months after the accident, I am finally discharged from the Royal Talbot rehab center. I've achieved what I set out to do, and then some. After walking out the hospital's front door, I will use my prostheses only once more before heading to Tasmania for the climb. I want to use them at home, away from the hospital, in "real life." And it feels incredible sitting in the backyard, pulling each leg on, one at a time. It was one thing to walk around the hospital—but now I'm at home, walking again in the place where I learned to walk as a child. I stand cautiously, adjust my belt, then step carefully across the uneven pink and gray paving stones outside the back door. Once on the concrete driveway I feel much safer. I can sense Mom and Dad watching me, and I imagine how they must feel.

Looking over to them, I call, "So. What do you reckon?"

Dad, standing now, walks toward me, reaching out.

"Mate . . ." his voice breaking. "I've wanted to do this for such a long time," he cries, his face against mine as we hold each other.

Tears stream down my face. "I love you, Dad."

────── ROCKY MOUNTAINS ──────

I first left Australia in June 1990, flying to Los Angeles with four mates. Doug (Dig), Dirk (Dirty), and Pete had been planning their trip for quite a while. We were all into fast cars (and bikes in Dig's case) and parts were dirt cheap in the U.S. at the time. Dave wasn't really interested in the car side of things. He just wanted to see a bit of the States and have a good time. Me, I just decided one night that I should join them—like Dave, not so much for the shopping (though I did end up buying a heap of car parts I never used) but to see something of the world.

I felt like I needed a change. I wasn't happy with my life and where I was headed. I had a well-paid job in the engineering department of the Gas & Fuel Corporation, designing metering systems for commercial and industrial consumers. But I didn't enjoy being stuck in an office all day, wearing a collar and tie. As I joined the other sheep on the train every morning and night, I knew there had to be more to life than that; at least, I hoped there was. I was living the life of the "weekend warrior," living for Friday night and drinking my way through the weekend, only to start the cycle all over again each Monday morning.

The thing that scared me was that I was good at it—really good. I figured that joining the guys on their trip would be the catalyst for making a change, and that when they all began to make their way back to Australia after a couple of months, I would stay. I don't believe in sitting around waiting for things to happen. I wanted to get out there and see what sort of a life I could create for myself. So I put in an application for twelve months' leave without pay, which was a common practice in the public service in those days. It was rejected, so I applied for six months. When that was rejected, I arranged a meeting with my supervisor. He offered me six weeks, my accrued annual leave.

"Forget it, I'm out of here," I replied without hesitation, and handed in my resignation.

Some of my colleagues tried to talk me out of my decision, focusing on how I should at least stay for another two years to receive my ten-year service leave.

"Yeah, right! I'm not looking forward to being here for another two weeks, let alone two years!" I looked around the building: I was surrounded by people that had been playing this game for, in some cases, twenty or thirty years.

Do you really want to do that?

Not everyone responded negatively to my quitting. Some of my closest workmates confided to me, "I wish I had done that when I was your age. It's too late for me now," which I agreed with at the time but don't anymore. It's never too late. Life is too short.

For two months, we partied our way across the States, traveling southeast from Los Angeles, through Arizona, across to Georgia and Louisiana, then northwest up through Tennessee to South Dakota. By the time we reached Yellowstone National Park, I needed a break. After two months of being stuck in the car with the same guys, I had to get out. I made a deal with Dig and Dirty (Pete and Dave had gone home to Australia by this stage) for them to do some sightseeing around the park so I could take off into the hills for a few days.

Inside the park's information office, I bought a map of the area and, with the help of the ranger on duty, selected a three-day walk into the

Rocky Mountains. I organized my food, said goodbye to Dig and Dirty, and took off. It felt so good to be getting some exercise—out in the fresh air with blue sky spread above me. The trail took me through a lightly wooded valley, the rugged peaks of the Rockies stretching out before me. Less than 5 kilometers (3 miles) from the road, I approached with curiosity what looked like a dead animal on the side of the track. Wow! *That thing looks like it's been chewed up and spat out,* I thought to myself, realizing immediately why. It had been! There are bears in Yellowstone National Park. I had been well aware of that when I left and had run through, in my mind, all the precautions to take. But I hadn't expected to come across something like this! Already!

I stepped back onto the trail, eyes scanning the tree line for any sign of movement. Seeing nothing, I quickly moved on, constantly checking in every direction, my heart pounding.

From that moment on, I stayed constantly on full alert. I'd never had to worry about anything more than snakes in the bush before (well, maybe mosquitoes and leeches)—*but bears?* This was an entirely new playing field.

After setting up camp that night, I cooked dinner quickly. Eating in the firelight, I felt like a crow on a roadside carcass, ready to leap up and abandon my meal at a second's notice. I froze solid when I thought I heard movement in the darkness. Then *craaack* came the sound of something big moving through the trees directly in front of me. Jumping to my feet and backward at the same time, I held my breath, my heart racing. With eyes like dinner plates, neck craned forward, I peered into the night. My body reacted with instinct, twisting to face the other way, ready to run. I frantically scanned the trees, looking for one to climb. *Don't run! Remember, you're not supposed to run!*

Snap! I swung around quickly, back to face the sound. *Shit! What is that? Please don't come any closer.*

Snap! Crack! Whatever it was, it was circling the fire. I slowly backed away, moving with the noise, keeping the fire between us as I constantly glanced over my shoulder, looking for the closest tree. I felt like I was still holding my breath, tensing my chest to stay quiet. Staring into the dark where the noise had come from, I waited for the signal that would send me running for a tree. *I know I'm not supposed to, but if that bear comes for me, I'm running like hell!*

For what seemed an eternity, I held off from making a move, until . . . *Am I imagining things, or is it moving away?* I strained my ears to listen. Sure enough, the noises were headed away from me now, until the sounds of movement faded into the distance.

Certain that whatever it was, bear, moose, or something else, it was gone, for now, I sprang into action, adrenaline surging through me. All the food, including my half-eaten dinner, went straight into a bag and into my pack. I had already thrown a rope over a high branch away from my tent and now I quickly tied my pack to it. I was hoisting it up when I remembered something I'd read the previous day, something about a bear being able to detect the smell of food in your clothes after you've cooked in them. *Shit!* I wasn't taking any chances. I stripped off and stuffed my clothes into the pack. Naked, I hoisted my pack into the tree, tied it off, and scampered into the tent.

I lay absolutely still, my heart skipping a beat with every sound outside. I felt so scared, so vulnerable. For the first time in my life, I felt what it was like to be on a lower rung of the food chain, felt the fear that man must have felt for thousands of years as he took shelter in caves or in a grass hut on the savannah, trying to keep out of reach of animals that wanted to kill him to survive. Turning the clock back to a time before we had conquered all our predators, I felt what it was like to be hunted, to be a true part of nature, without the protection, the security of what I've come to call "the plastic bubble" we all live comfortably inside.

To Surf, or Not to Surf . . .

Using the fit ball and the wobble board for balancing practice at the Talbot gave me an idea. And the time has finally come for me to try it out. Deirdre showed no hesitation when I mentioned heading down to the coast—she jumped at the chance to avoid studying for a few days. Now, the sun is beating down from a clear blue sky, the hot summer air lashing our faces through the open windows, as we speed down The Great Ocean Road.

I want to test my buoyancy in saltwater, to feel what it's like to swim in the ocean instead of up and down the length of a pool. But most of all, I want to surf. I felt like I was surfing whenever I sat on that Swiss ball at the Talbot, but the time has come to try the real thing. I've borrowed a boogie board from Stuart Tripp and can't wait to get it in the water.

As we pull in to the car park at Point Roadknight beach, Anglesea, the sea before us couldn't look more perfect. Clear blue water with gentle 1-meter (3.5-foot) waves fills the bay before us. A concrete boat ramp straight into the water makes it easy to get in, allowing me to wheel right down to the water's edge. I park the chair, then shuffle the remaining distance on my bum into the water that's lapping at the ramp's end. The swell threatens to unbalance me, so I stretch out in 30 centimeters (1 foot) of water and lunge forward.

The cold water brings every pore of my skin to life, invigorating me instantly. I swim out into deeper water, then just float, rising and falling with the swell. Swimming in the ocean has always been one of my favorite things, one of life's simplest pleasures. I thought I'd lost it forever. The feeling now, of claiming back another part of my life, is incredible. I try catching a few waves, body surfing. It's to no avail, the sea is too flat in the partly sheltered bay. *Never mind. We've got all day.*

Farther along the coast, we stop at Eastern View, a beach I have come to since childhood. The surf is much bigger here, the beach almost empty. I reach into the back of the car and pull out the boogie board, which Deirdre carries down to the beach while I nearly bust my gut pushing the wheelchair through the sand. I've let most of the air out of my tires, but I still have to give it everything I've got to get over the dune onto harder sand. I push myself to just short of the water's edge, then jump out, dragging the boogie board behind me by the ankle strap (*Mmmm. A lot of good that's going to do me.*)

The bigger, stronger waves make it difficult even to get into the water. The first one knocks me straight over; so does the second, as soon as I get back up again. I flop onto my stomach and crawl my way through the shallow water by clawing at the sandy bottom and pulling myself along, but I'm not fast enough and the next wave catches hold of the board (I'm hanging onto the ankle strap), carrying me back toward shore. I must look pretty funny floundering around like this in 30 centimeters of water.

I start again, this time gaining ground quickly, working out a way to get through the breakers. I have to hug the board as the waves hit me— I can't paddle through them like I once did. Every time I try, the board slides out from underneath me. After what seems like an eternity, I get out past the breaking waves and slump over the board to rest. *This is bloody hard work!*

As I wait for the right wave, I try to get myself balanced on the board, but it keeps shooting out from under me. *This is bloody ridiculous!* What I need is some surfboard wax. The board's plastic surface is too slippery against my chest; the fabric of my wetsuit gains no purchase on it. I'm not going to find any wax out here, though. As the next wave rolls toward me, I turn and begin paddling, almost matching its speed before it breaks behind me and knocks me straight off the board. I tumble along with the wave, getting completely trashed, coming up gasping for air in the foam. I decide I've had enough. I drag myself up the beach, disappointed but not shattered. I know that, with some grip on the board, I can do better.

As the weeks pass and my swimming improves, I start thinking more and more of an ocean race I swam about ten years ago—the Pier to Pub swim at the coastal vacation town of Lorne, two hours west of Melbourne on The Great Ocean Road. I decide as soon as I can swim the race distance of 1.2 kilometers (.75 mile) in the pool, I'll sign up for it. Before long I'm swimming 1.6 kilometers (1 mile) just to make sure I'm ready. Deirdre is keen to swim it too, so we begin training in earnest.

The race is held on January 10, 1998. It has been nine months since the accident, and a huge support team of family and friends have come down to Lorne to watch the race. I wheel down to the starting line in my chair, then jump out and shuffle into the water with the other competitors. Everyone is jostling for position (all 732 of us) when the gun goes off. It's like being in a washing machine for the next five minutes, all of us bunched together, each of us trying not to get swum over the top of.

Eventually, as the crowd disperses somewhat, I'm able to find a rhythm, which I maintain until the sandy bottom appears again as I near the shore.

In the final leg, as the other swimmers alongside me stand up in the shallow water and begin running toward the beach, I keep swimming, pulling myself along the sandy bottom when the water becomes too shallow to swim in. Waves break over me as I sit up in the water and shuffle up the beach on my backside. Per spots me and comes to my aid with the wheelchair. The first time I swing myself up to get in it, my arms give way and I crash down heavily onto the sand. The second time, I make it and begin pushing as hard as I can. I feel the stares of the on-lookers, but I'm concentrating totally on getting to the finish line. As the sand becomes softer where it has been churned up by so many swimmers funneling in to the finishing flags, I have to get out of the chair again. I cross the finish line on my bum to cheers of support from the crowd. I've reclaimed another part of my life, finishing in twenty-three minutes and one second—faster than my 1987 time (which shows what a bad kick I must have had) and 473rd in my age group, leaving 259 competitors to deal with the fact that they've been beaten by a guy with no legs. I feel on top of the world, like for the first time I've proven that my disability won't hold me back. In the water, it doesn't matter that I have no legs. Nobody knows—until I get to the shoreline that is.

Cradle Mountain can't come along fast enough. I'm hungry for it.

The following day finds a group of us, all nursing horrendous hang-overs, back at Eastern View Beach. I have a block of surfboard wax with me this time and I'm determined to redeem myself. Spurred on by Bun-yip (Andrew Bryant, a good friend of mine from Queensland's Sun-shine Coast), who has a backward bodysurfing style that has to be seen to be believed, I catch three decent waves. Riding them in to shore, I feel like the first surfer ever to do so.

Cradle Mountain

It's with both excitement and trepidation that I drive into Cradle Valley on the cold Thursday afternoon of January 29, 1998. Low cloud shrouds the peaks and a misty rain forms a soft haze, creating an otherworldly atmosphere. In my car with me are Cate Weate and Michael Croll. I spent a lot of time with Cate in the Tarkine and feel good about having her with me on this trip. I have just picked up Michael (who I met through Christine and Ebi, and visited often while living in Weldbor-rough) from his home in the state's northeast. Lisa and Per, who both wanted to see more of Tasmania since visiting me in Weldborough, are in their car behind us. Keen to climb the mountain with me, they've come across on the same ferry, though unfortunately they'll have to leave early due to work commitments. Arriving at the park entrance, we park outside the main office.

Wheeling into the building, I feel suddenly confronted by my sur-roundings. The whole place is set up for hikers, to provide information and recommend trails. I can't help thinking that people are looking at me, wondering what I'm doing here. With some hesitation, I wheel up to the counter, where a ranger stands. His badge says, "Peter."

"G'day mate. I've got a hut booked under the name of Macdonald, for tonight."

"You must be the bloke that's going to climb the mountain, hey?" he replies.

I almost blush with relief. For some reason I've been thinking that people might laugh when I mention my intentions, that they'll give me the look that says, "Oh, the poor thing. He thinks he can climb a moun-tain. Isn't that terrible?" I feel like a coiled spring, like a jack-in-the-box just waiting to burst out and surprise everyone. I hate the thought of projecting the stereotypical image of the helpless cripple, just by being in a wheelchair. People have no idea what I'm capable of. I gain strength from Peter's positive response.

"I surely am," I reply confidently, smiling.

"That's going to be pretty impressive if you get up there, mate. I've been around in my time, seen some amazing things. If you can get up there and can tell me what's up there when you get back, I'll make up one of our new certificates for you," he says, brimming with enthusiasm.

"I'll get up there. Don't you worry about that," I reply. "It will make things easier if the weather clears up a bit, though."

Although it's technically still summer, Tassie runs to its own schedule. Storms have been lashing the state over the previous few days and, though the wind has died down somewhat, it remains bitterly cold. Up on the plateau it will be colder still.

Leaving ranger Peter, we get back into the cars and drive the winding road through the valley to Waldheim. Gustav Weindorfer built the first hut here in 1912. He was a man who recognized the beauty of being in the wild, of gaining spiritual rejuvenation by being in the wilderness. I wonder what he'd think if he could see his valley now. His dream of Cradle Mountain being "a national park for the people" has certainly come to fruition.

The rain is heavier as we pull up outside the hut. Moving inside quickly, Per sets about lighting a fire. He and Lisa are freezing, the notorious Tasmanian weather having taken them totally by surprise.

"I'd hate to see you here in winter!" I joke, having a go at them.

We eat a huge bowl of pasta each, and are settling back to relax when there's a knock at the door. Through it walks Eddie Storace, complete with a bottle of port!

"Eddie! Me old mate!"

"Wazza! You old bastard!" he greets me warmly in return.

Eddie and I met through our involvement in the Tarkine campaign, and I spent a lot of time with him and his partner, Helen, at their home in Sisters Beach on the northwest coast of Tasmania. I've been in the bush with Eddie only once, but what a trip it was. The pair of us, along with two others (Kai and Bo), spent four days cutting a trail through 15 kilometers (9 miles) of rugged bush carrying 20 kilograms (44 pounds) of rapid-set cement (it's a long story!) . . . and Eddie thought he'd been invited for a casual hike.

I haven't seen Eddie since leaving Tassie nearly two years ago, which means he hasn't seen me since the accident, a situation that always feels weird. I go through the same feelings of awkwardness every time I meet an old friend like this, apprehensive within myself as to how they'll respond, fully aware of the shock it must be to see someone so physically changed. Thankfully, Eddie, like most others, quickly realizes something that has struck me, too: that, *hey, it's still me.* I'm just two feet shorter.

The only thing missing now is the news crew from the Melbourne-based TV station GTV9, which was to meet us here at the hut. A reporter from the station is interested in running a story on the climb, and I figure the publicity won't do any harm. Right now though, they're nowhere to be seen.

I try not to think about it too much, deciding that they'll turn up in the morning if they are still in the state. I finish packing the rest of my gear. All the food has been measured out and allocated to individual packs. We've double-checked our stoves and first-aid gear. We're ready to go. But as I slide into my sleeping bag, my mind races at the thought of the next day's journey. I ask myself, *What are you getting yourself into here? Do you really know what you're doing?* I drift off to sleep with mixed feelings, both anxious and excited at the prospect of getting started. I know I'm ready, that it's now or never. I know I can do it. *Or do I?*

The next day begins slowly—I feel so snug in my sleeping bag that I refuse to admit I'm awake at first, prolonging the inevitability of facing the brisk Tasmanian morning. It seems too early to get up. I let myself believe this for a while, until I begin thinking of the day ahead. Then I feel a sense of urgency. Out of the bag and dressing quickly, I rouse the others. They've all been lying there like me, waiting for someone else to move first.

"C'mon, get up!" I call out in mock order. "Let's get going!"

Through the cabin window we're greeted by a rather grim looking day, shrouded in low cloud. This is pretty typical for early morning in this part of Tassie, but we have the added unwelcome element of steady, drizzling rain. Early morning cloud is often dispersed as soon as the mid-morning sun touches it, but this drizzle could easily stay with us all day.

I've known all along that, if it's going to rain, it would be nice if it rains on the first day, rather than the second. I really need fine weather for the summit attempt, as any rain will make the dolerite boulders slippery. Bad weather below will make the trip uncomfortable, possibly even miserable, but it won't stop me from continuing. I've already decided that if we do strike bad weather up at Kitchen Hut, at the foot of the mountain, I'll wait it out there. It will then be in the lap of the gods as to whether I make it to the top or not. I can only wait as long as those helping me are prepared to stay.

As soon as we eat breakfast, I ask Lisa if she can drive back to Cradle Mountain Lodge to try and find the news crew. The rest of us move the vehicles down to the car park, then make last-minute adjustments to our packs. Gore-Tex-clad day-trippers eye me suspiciously, surely wondering what the hell I'm up to.

My pack lies under the seat of my wheelchair, strapped to the frame. I fixed it there weeks before to give me a chance to get used to the extra weight. Inside is my sleeping bag, Therm-a-rest, all my clothing, a flashlight . . . basically everything except my stove, tent, and food.

I push up and down the potholed gravel road, trying to keep moving to stay warm. Rolling downhill, I'm surprised at how tightly I have to grip the push-rims to keep control of the chair. My hands are freezing already and we haven't even reached the trail. I wonder how I'm going to do when I strike a tough stretch of the trek, whether I'll be able to push on through it with my hands weakened like this.

It's time to sign our intentions into the logbook, located in a little wooden shelter, partially sided, with a roof offering minimal but much appreciated protection from the bitter wind. I hold my hands up to my mouth and cup them together, blowing warm air over them, then rubbing them together and blowing on them again. I have to get them warm before I can write anything. As I turn from signing off my entry, Lisa steps into view, heading our way with a couple of guys looking very much like a film crew. *Excellent. They've made it.*

I wheel over to greet them. "How is it going, guys? I thought we'd lost you."

"So did we. When we didn't hear from you by 9 PM last night, we thought the whole thing might have been called off," one of them answers, sounding a bit put out.

"No chance of that, mate," I reply. "We got here a bit later than expected and thought, well, you guys know where we are. We'll let you come to us. Looks like you guys thought the same thing. Anyway, I'm Warren Macdonald. You must be Nick?"

"Sorry, yes. Nick Coe. And this is Simon, our sound man." He introduces the guy with the furry microphone, then the cameraman.

With the introductions over, I'm keen to get moving, happy now that things are falling into place.

"Ready when you are," Nick replies. He's wearing a pair of denim jeans, which tells me he hasn't done a lot of hiking or climbing before. I don't envy him. He's going to be pretty uncomfortable in those if this drizzle keeps up.

We make our way up the road to the trailhead, the beginning of what is probably Australia's best-known hike. Known as "the overland track," the trail continues for 80 kilometers (50 miles) through some of the most spectacular terrain in the country. We will be hiking the first 6 or 7 kilometers (4 or 4.5 miles) of the trail before splitting off toward Cradle Mountain. It has been two years since I was last here, on a day trip to the summit of Cradle. I was standing on two legs that day, legs that I *had* only ten months ago.

OK. *You can do this. Let's go!*

I put myself into a mono and begin descending the steep trail. I have a seat belt of sorts (a length of webbing that runs behind my seat and Velcros together at my waist) and this gives me some sense of security, but the trail is quite slippery. However, this quickly becomes the least of my worries when I reach the top of a flight of forty wooden steps cut into the trail. Hesitating at the top, the news team's camera rolling beside me, I decide *hey, I'm OK with five steps; I've done five plenty of times before. Forty is just five steps, eight times in a row* . . . and with that I pop into a mono and begin dropping down one step at a time.

Everything is going according to plan until I realize, with a sinking feeling, that the steps are not quite level. Every time I bounce down to the next one I shift a centimeter (.25 inch) to the left. Eventually, with nowhere else to go (I can't drop the front wheels again while on steps or I'll tumble out the front), I bounce straight off the steps, tumbling sideways into the button grass on the trailside. I've fallen only a third of a meter (1 foot) and I'm not hurt, but I feel like a total fool. I can just imagine the news crew, still filming, thinking, "this guy has dragged us all the way down here to film him climb a mountain, and we're not even 100 meters (330 feet) from the car and he's out of his chair." It's far from an ideal start.

My laughter reassures everyone that I'm OK. *So this is going to be more interesting than I thought!*

My seat belt is holding me into the chair, but I'm wondering whether that is a good thing. Undoing it, I slide out of the chair and climb back onto the boards. There will be so many unknown factors on this trip. I've been able to plan only so far, given that I haven't been able to find anyone who has done any off-road work in a wheelchair before. This will be a case of tackling each new problem as it arises, and working out a way around it.

Strapped back into my chair, I start again. I soon come to a drop that I know is too big. I'll fall out of my chair for sure if I attempt it. Undoing my seat belt, I climb out again and shuffle around it on my hands and bum, then ease back into the chair again until the next obstacle. Slowly, ever so slowly, we cross the plain this way, with me continuously in and out of the chair. The hooded figures of those supporting me stand patiently behind me as the cold wind sweeps misty rain across the plain.

Nobody says much. I think everybody knows, privately, the enormity of what we've set out to achieve. I wonder what else they are thinking, though, if they can even begin to imagine what this must be like for me, for someone who was at his best when walking reduced to this, shuffling along the ground like some kind of sideshow freak. I push these negative thoughts to the back of my mind, telling myself, *One step at a time. That's all you have to do.*

Stopping often to rest, I take in the landscape. This is such a beautiful place. A lot of Tasmanians discount it because of what it has become: a tourist destination. It certainly is that, but not without good reason; and that reason is why I'm here, tourists or no tourists. It is truly spectacular.

After an hour of relatively flat boardwalk, we begin climbing the first of the moraines, following alongside and above Crater Creek before entering the first section of rain forest. Myrtle and sassafras form a canopy over our heads, the dark forest around us is covered in a blanket of moss. The damp smell of the trees hangs in the very air. This is what I've come here for. This is why I've been so enchanted with Tassie since first arriving: the timelessness, the almost magical feeling evoked by being in a place that feels so primeval.

Climbing the pine staircase, I lean forward over each step before swinging my body up and onto the next. I feel strong, actually preferring these steeper sections as I feel I'm really achieving something in gaining altitude, rather than just shuffling along the ground. Climbing is what I've trained for.

Onward and upward we continue, until I hear excited voices up ahead. I know they can see the lake now, but not just the lake. I know what it is that has them going. They've just come face to face with the escarpment of Marion's Lookout—a seemingly sheer wall that rises 200 meters (660 feet) above the surface of Crater Lake. I think this is the first moment that Lisa has grasped the full extent of this trip—that this is in fact a mountain (as Daphne had pointed out), not just a sloping hill.

"How do we get up there?" she asks.

"See to the left there," I point. "The track zigzagging up the face?"

"Yeah?" she replies hesitantly, almost in disbelief.

"That's where we're going. That track will take us onto the top of the plateau," I continue confidently, butterflies rising in my stomach at the sight. The climb now seems five times higher than I recall from my last visit here.

The news crew does a quick interview with me beside the lake before leaving us for the day, the plan being for them to return to the comfort of Cradle Mountain Lodge, then catch up with us again in the morning at Kitchen Hut. We wish them well, then huddle into Gustav Weindorfer's old boat shed on the lakeshore for some lunch. Trangias boil away as we make the first of a number of coffees—accompanied by large quantities of chocolate, of course.

I feel strong physically; but extremely vulnerable at the same time, sitting in a small three-sided shack, hours away from civilization, with no legs. There is no quick escape route for me and I think that's what is playing on my mind more than anything: the thought that if something does go wrong, I'll have to rely on others to get me out. I'd never experienced that before Hinchinbrook. I'm not in a hurry to experience it again.

Leaving the relative security of the hut, we make our way around the lake, climbing gently toward the escarpment. I hop out of the chair. Per, Michael, and Eddie disassemble it for the ascent. Carrying it will be no easy task for them, as the track is mainly loose scree. It's difficult walking at the best of times, let alone shouldering a pack whilst carrying a wheelchair. But all I can concentrate on is the next step directly in front of me, cut into the mountainside and reinforced with pine boarding; each one is a new hurdle to overcome. Some, I have to lift my bum up onto as I hold onto the sides, bracing myself with my forearms. Others are too steep to be negotiated this way, and I have to slide up on my chest before sitting up. I have the feeling that, if I do fall backward, without legs I won't be able to stop myself from tumbling. I haven't proven this theory yet and I'm in no big hurry to, either. So I move carefully, one step at a time up the steep slope until, finally, after an hour or so, I reach the top. There in front of me, its jagged lines cut into the horizon, looms my destination.

"Wogsy! That's huge!" Lisa exclaims.

"It is, isn't it? Check it out!" I reply, happy to just sit and look at it for a while. Then, breaking the silence: "All right. Kitchen Hut's not far from here. We'd better keep moving."

Moving across the plateau is made easier by the fact that I can see the mountain most of the time. The track between Marion's Lookout and Kitchen Hut rolls over a gentle arc, occasionally cut by creeks running down toward the lakes below. Each time the track dips down into one of these creeks, I lose sight of the hut, which takes away my urgency to keep moving. That said, at some points when I *can* see the hut, I feel like I'm not making any progress at all. My wrists are aching; they're taking most of the strain. I alternate between moving on my palms—which is harder on my wrists—and using my knuckles in a clenched fist. This is easier on my wrists but very hard on my knuckles, especially when moving over scree. My forearms also burn with each forward step, taking my full weight as I swing my body over them.

The sun sinks lower as we approach Kitchen Hut, the last 100 meters (330 feet) seeming to take forever. My ambling into the camp draws a chorus of whoops and yelps. Eddie hugs me fiercely: "Wazza! Mate!"

Cate stands behind me, hugging me tight. "You're a legend, Waz." I feel like I've won the first half of a marathon.

I made it! I've made it to Kitchen Hut!

It's now 6 PM. It has taken us all day to get here but we have made it. I'm so glad to see everyone sharing in my excitement. I still haven't gotten used to the idea of people having to stop and wait for me every five minutes; it makes me feel very uncomfortable. Sitting with my back against the hut on a slab of stone, I look up at the peak before me, clouds partly obscuring my view.

I feel emotionally overwhelmed as the enormity of what is happening sinks in. *We are on the mountain!* Everything I have worked toward over the last few months is coming to fruition, at the same time my lingering doubts are beginning to fade. The fears I've had over whether or not I've aimed too high, my worry that people are just feeling sorry for me for being so delusional as to think this is even possible, these begin to dissipate. Dissipate, but not disappear altogether . . .

I watch the shadows—growing longer before my eyes—creep across the face of the mountain in front of me. Black clouds are gathering in the east, but you can never really tell what the weather might do up here. Inexperienced hikers still get caught out on Cradle, even in the middle of summer. There have been a number of deaths up here over the years, mostly trekkers who underestimated the mountain's changeable weather and who were unprepared for the worst. *We're not there yet. I've done* OK *so far, but anything could happen still.*

With the sun sinking into the horizon, I sit back and rest while the others prepare the evening meal. No sooner have we eaten than my sleeping bag beckons. It has been such a long day. My aching body needs some rest, though my mind is still racing at what I've achieved, at what lies ahead. But as I lie in my sleeping bag on the hut's wooden floor, my legs just won't warm up. There is too much air space in the bag where my legs used to be, making it difficult to retain body heat. Using a length of nylon webbing, I tie the end of the bag off, effectively reducing its length. I warm up in no time.

Drifting off to sleep, I feel like I've regained something more today, something I'd prided myself on before the accident: the ability to take myself out of my comfort zone and to learn from the experience. Throughout this day, I've been well within my comfort zone as I *used to* know it. What the accident has done though, I now realize, is reduce that comfort zone—which I've spent my whole life expanding—to the size of what can best be described as a tight-fitting wetsuit. When I woke up in the hospital, I had no control over anything outside my own skin, and over the months since I've worked to expand that through learning how to live within my new boundaries. What's happening right now is something entirely different. I'm reclaiming not just the ability to live inside the "plastic bubble" but my ability to live outside it as well, and that's huge. It's with that thought that I fall asleep, totally at peace with myself for one of the few times in my life.

The cold keeps us snuggled in our bags again the next morning. I've never really been one of those up-at-the-crack-of-dawn hikers, the type that drives everybody nuts in communal huts by stomping around in heavy boots at 5 AM. I prefer a more leisurely start. But hearing Cate stir beside me, I know it's time to face the day. It can't be more than 4 or 5°C (39 or 40°F) as I shuffle out of my bag quickly and dress in all the clothes I have with me. Opening the door of the hut presents me with a glorious sight: a clear blue sky and not a cloud in sight. *The gods are smiling on us!*

The Summit

We are all in such high spirits. So much hinges on the weather this day, and it looks like we are in luck. If the weather turns bad, it will mean having to postpone any summit attempt until it clears. At best, we can afford to be holed up for a day, possibly two. I can't expect the others to stay any longer than that, and I can't stay here alone.

Sitting outside the hut in the morning sun, two figures appear across the plateau, making their way toward us. One of them is the unmistakable form of Brian Hall (built like a rugby player), the other, his wife, Val.

It feels so good to see Brian again, especially in this setting. This is how he first came to know me: in the outdoors, at my best. And this is how he is seeing me again now. I'd thought I might feel weakened seeing Brian, that he might feel sorry for me seeing me as I am now. But thankfully, I was wrong. He respected me as a hiker, knowing it was something I did well. Seeing him now, like this, feeling his admiration for me in having got here, makes me feel so much stronger. He has that quality: to bring out the best in people. He and Val have taken the weekend off to see me reach the top.

As we reacquaint ourselves, Lisa and Per prepare themselves for their push to the top. They are booked on the 4 PM ferry from Devonport back to Melbourne this afternoon. They'll have to leave now if they are to make the summit in time. I wish them luck as they make their way to the mountain's base.

Ten minutes later, another two figures approach from Marion's Lookout. This time it's Meagan Doherty, a reporter from the *Examiner* (a Tasmanian newspaper based in Launceston), who wrote a story on my involvement in the Tarkine campaign when I first returned to Tassie after my accident. I was impressed with the results after having been savaged by the Tasmanian media during Tarkine times. With her is Jeremy Smith, a photographer, who we discover later is quite an experienced climber.

No sooner are we done with the introductions than another group appears with two smaller members out in front, running toward us: Ebi and Ian, with their respective sons, Seppi and Kieran. This is the first time on Cradle Mountain for all of them. Again, a reunion atmosphere takes over, but not for long. We have to get moving. The time is nigh, and I have a job to do.

Looking up at the mountain once more, bathed in sunlight, I lower my head and make my first shuffle forward over the earthen track. In places, the trail is cut through what would normally be knee-deep alpine heath. I have to turn and twist, dragging myself through it sideways. As

I climb the steadily steepening track, the earth gives way to what is known as "talus" and "scree"—rock fragments that have crumbled off the mountain, littering the slopes below (talus is usually big enough to be used as stepping stones; scree ranges from small to large pebbles). I'm forced to lift my bum higher to clear the rough ground. Onward and onward we climb, eventually stopping at a small spring for a granola break.

The day has a fairly relaxed atmosphere. Although I find the climb demanding physically, I have total confidence that I'm going to make it, which keeps me calm and relaxed mentally. As the hours pass, we find ourselves bathed in the sunshine of a perfect summer's day: not so hot as to make it unbearable, but not a cloud in the sky all the same. I chat with whoever is alongside me as we climb. With Brian, the conversation hinges on what other course members are doing with themselves these days, about what I'm doing in Melbourne now that my rehabilitation is over.

Eventually, the scree gives way to huge blocks of dolerite looming above me. I have to lie on my stomach to drag myself up and over each piece. Huge columns tower overhead; the remnants of those fallen make up the talus and scree below, dramatizing the trail's instability. As I gain height, the climbing becomes steeper, until eventually it's too steep for me to attempt without great risk of tumbling backward. Since I still don't know how I'll stop myself if I do fall back, it's about time to set up the first pitch of technical climbing.

Brian and Jeremy set up a top rope-bottom belay system, fixing a sling around a large boulder up above while I put on my harness. But as I get the OK to climb and began edging my way up the slab, a sudden uneasiness creeps over me, something I have successfully avoided until now.

My weight is pulling on this rock. If it comes loose, I'm underneath it.

The realization shakes me to the bone. I cringe deep within myself, momentarily reliving the Hinchinbrook experience, feeling the rock give way in my mind.

No, it couldn't! It couldn't happen again, could it?

I try to reassure myself that that isn't possible, that fate just could not be so cruel.

If it does come down, then so be it. It was just never meant to be.

I'm actually angry at the thought, the possibility that some god above could be so cruel as to let another rock fall on me. I'm almost issuing a challenge: *Go on, you wouldn't dare! Even you couldn't be so cruel.*

I reach for an edge and, once found, use it to pull myself up with one arm while I work the other beneath me to mantle myself forward. Then, lying flat on my stomach, I reach up to repeat the move, inching my way up toward the top of the boulder. At the top, I look over the edge to see a huge gap between myself and the next slab. *Shit, this is going to be interesting.*

I carefully get my hands into position, then lower my body down between the two slabs of rock, feeling so soft and vulnerable between the hard, rough stone. Once down in the gap, I begin the climb up the face of the next boulder. And so it goes for the next three hours until we reach the amphitheater just below the summit.

Running out of daylight now, it's clear that we need to get some gear up here for a night on the summit. We can't possibly make it up and down in the day as planned. Ebi, Ian, Eddie, and Michael volunteer to dash back down to the hut. Gathering all the available water bags, they take off at great speed, hoping to make it back in time for my arrival at the summit. I keep moving, finally arriving in the amphitheater I know is close to the top. It's like a huge hollow in the mountaintop, and we have to descend into it, then traverse above the gorge it drops into before we can climb steeply onto the main summit plateau.

It's damp in the amphitheater. Very little sun penetrates its confines, and a community of different plants live up here in the shadows. On both my previous visits there has been a patch of snow still hiding in the shadows, in the middle of summer. But the view from this saddle is spectacular, giving us our first lookout to the east, across to the Walls of Jerusalem and beyond, over seemingly endless rugged peaks, deep gorges, and lakes. My spirit soars at the sight and I feel the adrenaline coursing through my veins.

I'm almost there! I'm going to make it!

I'm now at the section I remember as being the most likely to give me trouble. The climb out of the amphitheater involves 5 to 6 meters (16 to 20 feet) of almost vertical rock. One section, of roughly 2 meters

(6.5 feet), is slightly overhung, enough for some members of our party to remove their packs before attempting it. Jeremy sets up this last pitch, belaying from below, with Brian encouraging me on from above.

Hauling myself up I still feel strong, even stronger as I sense the closeness of my goal. When I reach the overhang, I'm forced to climb the rope before reaching the top and scraping over the edge on my stomach. Brian is going off with excitement.

"Wazza! You're there, son!"

I untie from my harness and just sit at the edge, taking in the spectacular scenery, savoring the exhilarating feeling of being on a mountain again, my senses reeling, the sheer emotion of what I've been through to get here, how I never thought I'd get here again. Looking down onto the trail far below, it's hard to believe that I dragged myself over every centimeter, every stone of it.

A cool breeze sweeps across the plateau. I was protected from it while in the hollow, but now I need to move before it chills me. I remember this stretch to the summit's highest point. Made up of huge boulders of dolerite that have split and broken with the repeated freezing and thawing over thousands of years, it was tricky even on two legs. Huge cracks separate every boulder, some dropping into darkness with no indication of their depth. I imagine many a camera being dropped down into them, never to be seen again.

In some ways, crossing this sort of terrain is more difficult than actually climbing. With climbing, I feel that I'm achieving something with each pull upward. Moving up and down through these huge cracks seems to go on forever, seems to drag out the inevitable. It's almost as though the mountain is saying, "Uh-uh. You're not there yet." But I can see the summit marker most of the time, which spurs me on, though it disappears from view each time I have to drop into the next crack before continuing.

Guided constantly by Brian and Cate, I move closer and closer.

"This way, Wazza. It looks pretty dodgy over there, mate." They too have become accustomed to my capabilities and are beginning to appreciate that some things that might seem easy for me are actually very difficult.

A crowd has gathered around the summit marker now: the news crew, Jeremy and Meagan, Cate and Brian. I fight to keep the lump in my throat down, as tears well in my eyes behind my sunglasses. So many emotions seem ready to overwhelm me: sheer joy at having achieved something that, only six months before, seemed gone from my reach forever; the ability just to be out in nature, away from the picnic tables and car parks of the weekend picknickers; deep sadness at the reality of what has happened to me, what I am now. I know that this is it now, this is how hard it will be for me to get to the simplest of places; the sort of hiking that I'd surpassed years ago. At the same time, I feel forced to look at why I ever put myself into the wilderness in the first place, and especially now, like this.

Is it to feel that sense of achievement, that I've conquered a mountain or an inhospitable place? Is it to be able to come out and say, "It might have been tough, but I got through it OK"? Is it the physical and mental challenge? Or is it because of the enormous peace I feel when surrounded by nature, that all-encompassing feeling of being part of the world, able to stand back and see my place in it—which offers a glimpse into my very soul? Pushing these questions from my mind, I take a deep breath and move forward . . .

Shuffling the last few meters just as carefully as I have every step of the way . . . reaching out and grabbing the frame of the summit marker, I climb underneath it. Amidst the encouragement of everybody here, I can almost *feel* their support for me, their willing me on, in the air. Moving to the center of the frame, I sit with the trig plate between what remains of my legs and place a hand on it.

"That'll do me."

EPILOGUE

To say that the events recorded in these pages proved a major turning point in my life is something of a huge understatement. People ask me whether I think the accident provided me with direction, and, as such, was it a positive thing?

Make no mistake, getting around without legs is not easy, though at times I make it seem so. But I didn't *need* to lose my legs to become the person I am today.

I had already learnt that what we do with our lives is solely up to us; that we have to make things happen rather than sit and wait for them to come to us. The difference between now and then is that even though I knew this before, I was quite happy to soak up the sun in the meantime, something I find difficult to do now with my new sense of urgency regarding how long we're here for on this planet.

In climbing to the summit of Cradle Mountain, I reclaimed something of the life I had all but lost. But that reclamation kept me satisfied for only a very short space of time. No sooner had we returned to "civilization" than my mind began to turn over new possibilities. Twelve months following the events described in these pages, this willingness to "step outside" my comfort zone once again, after all I'd been through, led me on a journey to the summit of Australia's most challenging hike, Federation Peak. Accessible only to the hardiest of souls, Federation Peak lies smack dab in the middle of the South West Wilderness Area, a region protected by World Heritage status in the southwest corner of Australia's island state, Tasmania.

One of my reasons for taking on such a challenge was to prove a point. Years before, during the campaign to protect the Tarkine in the state's northwest, I (along with my friends) had been accused of being selfish and elitist in promoting the "locking up" of the area, effectively restricting access to "normal" people who "have the same right to be in there." These detractors claimed that, without the road, the area was accessible only to the young and fit. I wanted to show them, through my climb of Federation Peak, that such places are indeed accessible to those with enough passion and strength of will, and that by providing "instant" access, we lose the very quality that makes a place special to begin with—its *wildness*.

Yet reaching Federation Peak's summit (after an epic twenty-eight-day journey), whilst once again giving me a huge sense of accomplishment, only seemed to further ignite my burning ambition to discover just what somebody without legs might ultimately be capable of. That question seems to have been answered, for now anyway, with my ascent in February 2003 of Africa's tallest peak, Mt. Kilimanjaro (5,895 meters/19,340 feet). In 2003, I also managed to climb the Central Pillar route (W16) on Weeping Wall, 180 meters (590 feet) of classic waterfall ice in the Canadian Rockies, as well as the United States' tallest vertical rock face, El Capitan, in Yosemite National Park, California—which seems to indicate that, if anything, my taste for adventure has increased following my accident.

Long before Hinchinbrook, however, I had friends tell me I should write a book about the way I approached life: always open to adventure. But sharing such experiences was never something I took seriously until this story literally "fell into my lap." Initially, I began writing purely for personal reasons; it took quite some time before I realized the effect my story had on others. It seemed to provide inspiration to those grappling with this strange thing we call "life" and helped them put their own difficulties into perspective. Of course, if things had stayed as simple as me having that effect from a distance, by means of a collection of words on the page, it would have been easy, but one thing tends to lead to another.

Being asked to "stand up" in front of a room full of people and share my story both excited me and scared me witless. Luckily, I like a challenge, and I now gain tremendous satisfaction from helping others discover their full potential, something I could never have envisioned in my life prior to April 1997.

Traveling the world and sharing my story has become a way of life for me, with each journey opening new doors. One of those doors led me to Alberta, Canada, in October 2002, where I introduced Gary Caganoff's film *The Second Step* (the documentary of my Federation Peak climb) at the Banff Mountain Film Festival. At a party celebrating local climbing legend Barry Blanchard's Summit of Excellence award, I managed to lose my wheelchair (I tend to swap it for a "normal" chair whenever I can) to a woman named Margo Talbot, who some hours later realized somebody might be missing it.

Margo and I now live in Vancouver, B.C., just minutes from the Coast Mountains.

Warren Macdonald
July 2004

For up-to-date information on Warren's current adventures or to contact him in regard to his speaking services, visit www.warren-macdonald.com.

NOTE: For the record, Geert van Keulen *did* have a permit to climb Mount Bowen, along with a route description that had been issued to him in Townsville. Although I didn't have a permit myself, I justified my right to climb with Geert by the simple fact that basic hiking ethics warn against traveling alone.

I have accepted that what happened to me was an act of nature, and that I was simply in the wrong place, at the wrong time.

ACKNOWLEDGMENTS

I would like to sincerely thank:

Kathryn Mulders, for her belief in me and for exceeding my expectations in what I thought an agent could do for me.

Rob Sanders at Greystone, for enthusiastically jumping on my story, and Anne Rose, for the great work on the unenviable task of editing my scribbled notes into something readable. To Susan Rana, and everybody at Greystone; you know who you are.

Hanger Prosthetics, for their continued support, especially Randy Richardson, Kevin Carroll, and Chad Simpson.

Outdoor Research, in particular Dad Nordstrom and Todd Walton for your support in gearing me up to get out there.

Margo Talbot, for her love and support, and for teaching me how to climb ice.

Everybody at Queensland Emergency Services, for their role in my rescue, in particular Dany Portefaix, Greg Beer, Tim Kesteven, and Bill Johnstone.

Dr. Chip Jaffurs MD, for keeping me alive until we reached Cairns Base Hospital.

The staff who treated me well at Cairns Base Hospital, including: Surgeon Bill Clark, Dr. John Morgan, Dr. Lara Weiland, Dr. Katherine

Swanson, Roger (nurse)—and all of the others whose names have escaped me. The staff at the Royal Talbot Rehabilitation Centre.

My family, especially Mom and Dad for being there for me when I needed them most, and Auntie Elaine and Uncle Wal McCulloch for their support.

Belinda Wells, Natalie Dudding, Paul and Karen Wilson, the North East Highlands Forest Action Group, Steph Cahalan, Daphne Smith, Deidre McEwan, Harm Ellens, and Leanne Kennedy for your friendship and support.

Also:

Andrew Denton and Duncan Machin, Mountain Equipment (U.K.)

Matt Martin, Oakley Australia

Simon Head, Bogong Equipment (Melbourne, Australia)

David Edwards, Mont Adventure Equipment (Canberra, Australia)

John Liddell, Sonar Wetsuits (Melbourne, Australia)

Jonathan Lockhead, Intermedia Works (Melbourne, Australia)

Qantas Airways

Everybody who helped with my Cradle Mountain climb, in particular Brian Hall, Ian and Kym Matthews, Ebihard and Christine Haas, Michael Croll, Susie Aulich, Cate Weate, Lesley Nichlason, Jeremy Smith, Eddie Storace, and Lisa and Per Thomsen.

Last but not least, Geert van Keulen, for doing what he had to do and doing it well, and for his contribution in sharing his part of a remarkable story.